MW00999764

 # THE DIRTY APRON COOKBOOK

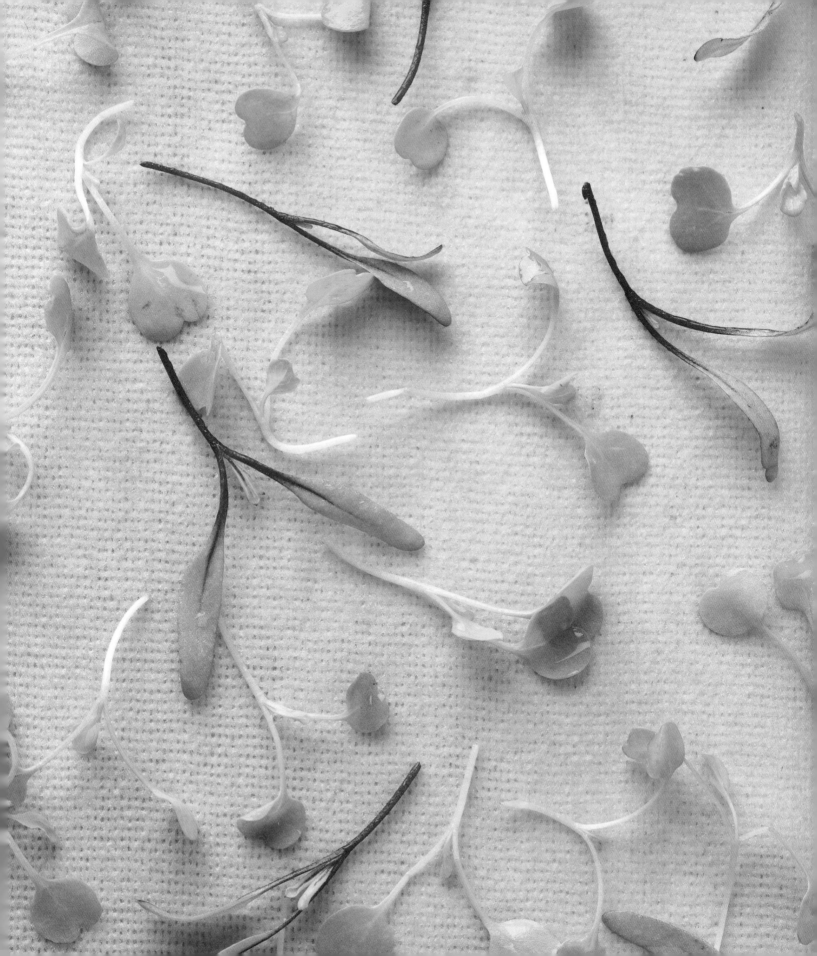

David Robertson

Foreword by **Vikram Vij**

THE DIRTY APRON COOKBOOK

Figure.1

Vancouver / Berkeley

To my two beautiful daughters, Chase and Dylan,
and to my amazing wife, Sara. You are the light of my
life, and I draw my strength and passion from all of you.

Cataloguing data available from Library and Archives Canada
ISBN 978-1-927958-17-9 (hbk.)

Writing by Kerry Gold
Editing by Lucy Kenward
Copy editing by Eva van Emden
Design by Peter Cocking
Photography by John Sherlock
Printed and bound in China by C&C Offset Ltd.
Distributed in the U.S. by Publishers Group West

Figure 1 Publishing Inc.
Vancouver BC Canada
www.figure1pub.com

CONTENTS

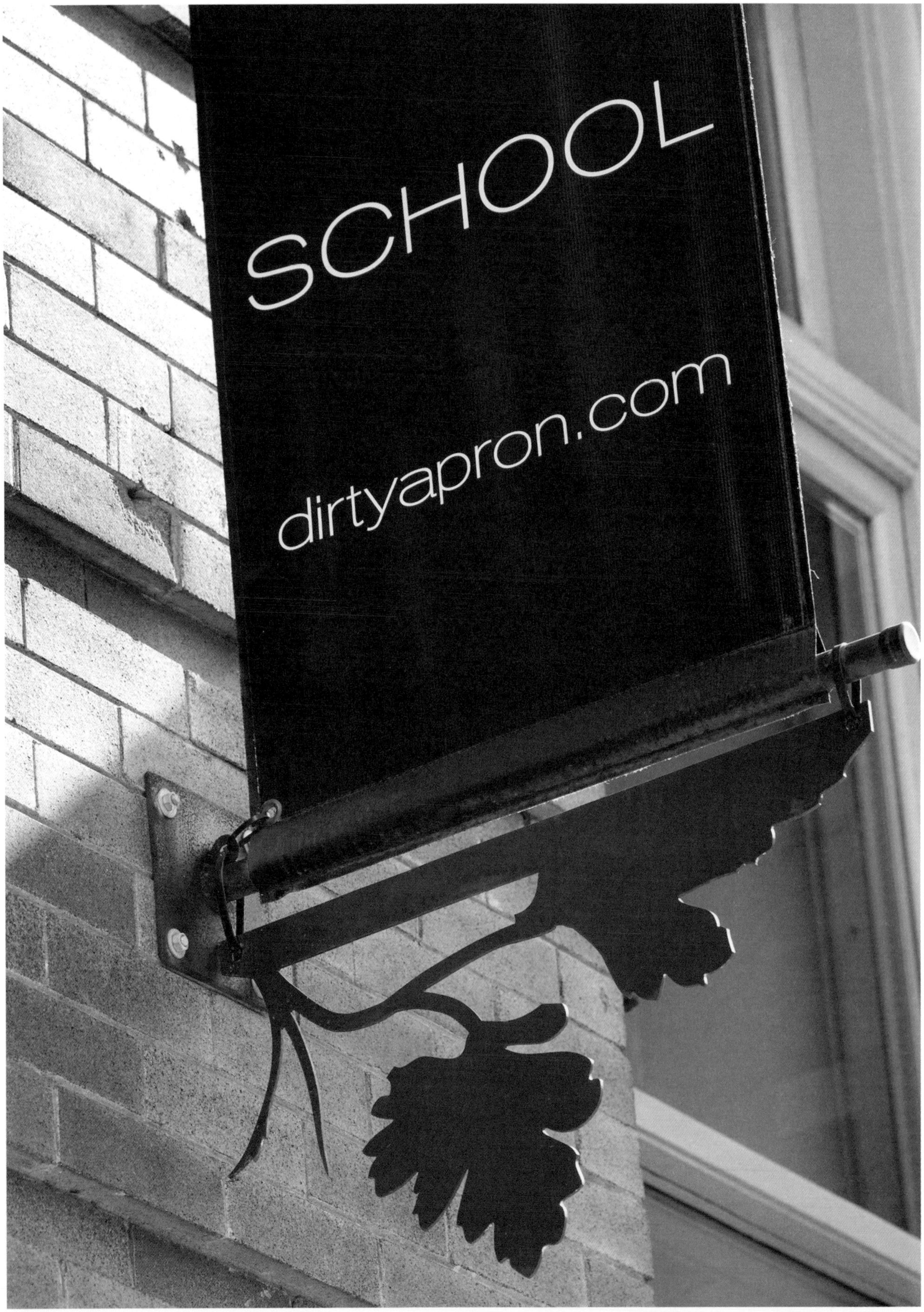
SCHOOL
dirtyapron.com

I have known Chef David Robertson for several years now because of this fabulous place called the Dirty Apron, where I have taught courses on cooking. For David and his staff, there is a commitment to teaching people about food, about cooking together, about how cooking can be fun and deeply rewarding—and about all the pleasures that go with cooking, which are many.

I really enjoy David's commitment to his profession and his way of thinking about food. On a personal level, I have also enjoyed working with David. He's always been an amiable and innovative chef who's there for his students.

And when you go to his deli, you see the food made with a lot of love and care. The place is funky and it's different; he doesn't run a regular lunch spot. Each and every sandwich, all the food, is made with the utmost attention to the ingredients, the flavours and the textures. He's a chef after my own heart.

For all these reasons, I would definitely recommend not only this cookbook but the Dirty Apron as a place where friends and family can gather for a great celebration of food.

And by the way, one of the best things about the Dirty Apron Cooking School is that you don't have to clean up. Somebody else does the cleanup for you.

VIKRAM VIJ · *Chef and Co-owner, Vij's, Rangoli and Vij's Railway Express*

Dear food lover, newbie cook and home cook extraordinaire: This book is for you.

My intention with this book is the same as with our classes at the Dirty Apron Cooking School—to teach you how to make delicious meals that could appear on the menu at any high-end restaurant. However, you'll learn how to prepare these meals without the need to possess oodles of technique, search out obscure or costly ingredients, or spend all day in the kitchen. Fine food shouldn't be elitist or mysterious. Cooking should be fun, joyous and rewarding.

Before we get started, let me tell you up front that the key to making great food is using fresh ingredients. That's non-negotiable. The other key is having a passion for it. Since you're reading this book right now, chances are pretty good that you're already a person who enjoys time in the kitchen. The cooking bug bit me early on in life, and it put me on a path that's been intensely challenging, exhausting, gruelling and hugely rewarding—the only possible career choice I could have made. I love to cook, and I love to teach, which is how the Dirty Apron Cooking School came to be.

My parents had a passion for food, and they made a big deal out of nightly dinners and soup-and-sandwich lunches. My father, Vernon, was a butcher, and every night he'd bring home cuts of meat: rib-eye steaks, pork chops and shanks. Suffice it to say that as a child I greatly enjoyed the advantages of my mother's cooking and my father's butchering skills. The stage was set for my career as a chef. Twenty years later, I am a classically trained French chef and, alongside my wife, Sara, and a great team, I run the Dirty Apron, which offers more than thirty different cooking classes.

I never expected to be a teacher, but in 2004, I was hired as the sous-chef at an exciting new restaurant called Chambar. We worked really hard to get Chambar on the map, and during my years there, not only did I cook, but I gave talks at food events, did media presentations and taught the odd class. Although teaching was something I'd never done before, it opened up a whole new world of possibility for me. I loved the interaction with students, and I could tell that my passion for food was inspiring them. Suddenly I found myself in love with the idea of being a passionate educator. Nico and Karri Schuermans, the owners of Chambar, agreed to go into business with me so we could open our own cooking school.

My friends thought I was crazy, giving up a great chef job to open a cooking school. This was 2008, the year the market crashed. My wife was pregnant. And

I had quit a good job. But I threw myself into the new venture. I went to the East Coast and attended a lot of cooking schools there, from the perspective of a student. I kept notes on what worked and what didn't. For example, I paid $190 for one class, and I was put into a group with eight other people. We followed the same recipe, and while I was cutting an onion, somebody else was chopping garlic. We found ourselves standing around a pot with one guy stirring. The instructor did the plating at the end. It was a fun class, but I didn't learn much about cooking because I didn't get enough opportunity to be hands-on. I knew what not to do.

As it turned out, the lousy economy didn't matter. Our timing couldn't have been better. People responded with overwhelming positivity to the idea of a cooking school. The Dirty Apron received a ton of media attention, and the popularity of our classes started to grow. Because most classes are offered at night, we launched a deli for the lunch crowd in August 2011. We make sandwiches, salads, hot comfort-food dishes and soups with the same exacting cooking techniques and passion that we teach at the school. As a result, we have our Dirty Apron diehards, and I've gotten to know them all. It's the food that bonds us. Cooking is a return to home, friends and family—the comfort we all crave when the rest of the world proves a challenge. Quite simply, it makes us feel good.

Since we opened our doors at the Dirty Apron in 2009, we've taught more than 40,000 students the basics of preparing a delicious multi-course meal. They arrive at our classes individually, or with a spouse or cooking buddy, and they end the evening on a high note—glowing not just because they've enjoyed a glass of fine wine but also because they've experienced the intense satisfaction that comes from making a superb meal. It's one thing to spend money on a great meal prepared by someone else—it's an entirely different feeling to create it yourself. Many of our students are astonished at how straightforward the process can be, once they understand the fundamentals of great cooking.

With this Dirty Apron cookbook, I want to share with you some of the most popular recipes that have come out of the school, as well as a few from our deli and catering menus. These recipes are flavourful and easy to make, and they illustrate basic cooking techniques and flavour combinations you can use in your own meals at home. I show you a thing or two about building layers of flavour to compose the perfect salad such as the Caramelized Fennel and Goat Cheese Salad (page 52),

NO SPRINGS

HONEST WEIGHT

COOKING

THE DIRTY APRON

N 540

HOME
sweet
HOME!

and you'll discover why the salad selection at our deli makes it tough for customers to choose. I love soups, especially hearty ones like our amazing Porcini Mushroom and Chestnut Soup (page 38), and I'll give you tips about how to create soups that don't disappoint. I'll teach you how to build the most delicious sandwiches, including our Braised Lamb Sandwich with Spiced Yoghurt (page 58), a true five-star meal between bread. For the big guns, I've included classic main dishes such as our Boeuf Bourguignon (page 132), Braised Beef Short Ribs (page 130), Crispy Seared Duck Breast (page 123) and Grilled Lamb Chops with Olive Tapenade Herb Crust (page 135). I'll show you how to make even an inexpensive cut of meat succulent, moist and flavourful. And if seafood intimidates you, you'll find some easy recipes that showcase the subtle flavour of fresh fish paired with ingredients that you might not expect, such as the Maple-Seared Scallops with Warm Chorizo and Kalamata Olive Ragout (page 101). As for the closer—dessert—even those of you who don't usually fuss with baked goods will be turning out homemade puff pastries, cakes, ice creams and sorbets and impressing friends and family. I highly recommend the Dirty Twixter Bars (page 144), a combination of my two favourite chocolate bars. With these recipes, I intend to take the intimidation factor out of cooking.

When I'm teaching at the Dirty Apron, I like to pass on all the little tricks and techniques I've picked up over the years. You'll find many of those tips in these pages along with suggestions for new ideas to play with. I call cooking "the new yoga." There was a time when no teenage boy would admit to having a fondness for cooking. Now when I teach kids' cooking camp, 60 per cent of my students are teenage boys who want to spend a week in the kitchen learning how to cook. That tells you something. It's become cool.

The Food Network and all those celebrity chefs are helping to generate a buzz and an appreciation of food. And people have taken a huge interest in where their food is sourced and how it's made. We travel more than ever. The way we look at food has completely changed. We are living in a food nation, and if you love the craft and the daily challenge of creating, there is no better time to be a cook, whether it's in a professional kitchen or at home cooking for guests. So let's get cooking.

MISE EN PLACE

Here's a bit of advice that will make your job in the kitchen so much easier. First off, get properly set up before you get down to the business of cooking. Nothing brings a happy cooking session to a grinding halt like realizing you're missing an essential component.

The French call the business of getting set up the *mise en place*, and, as fancy as that sounds, it's actually quite simple. It means, get your stuff out in front of you where you can easily access it. Read through the recipe, get out your equipment and utensils, etc., and assemble and measure your ingredients. If you'll need space in the fridge or freezer later, clear that space now. It's also the time to preheat the oven. When you've thought of everything in advance, and only then, can you get down to cooking.

At the school, students arrive at their stations and everything is measured out, already set up for them. I figure that in the few hours we have together, they should only have to focus on the actual cooking. At home you won't have that luxury, but here are a few things I always have in my pantry that you can use as a guideline for your own:

Good salt My go-to salts are *fleur de sel*, Maldon and kosher salt.

Hot spice I usually have something like Espelette chili pepper or smoked paprika on hand, for when a dish needs a kick.

Mustard I appreciate good mustard, and I have a variety, including a good Dijon and a grainy mustard.

Fresh herbs I always have parsley, chives and fresh thyme in the fridge.

Stock You'll find good homemade chicken stock in my freezer at all times. This is essential.

Olive oil I always have two kinds—extra-virgin olive oil for salads and garnishing, and a basic virgin olive oil for cooking at medium-low heat.

Unsalted butter I like to control the salt that goes into my dishes, so I make sure to have unsalted butter on hand.

Whipping cream To round out a soup or sauce with extra richness, I often use whipping cream. Look for 35 per cent milk fat for that richness.

Cheese My fridge is never without cheese—you'll find a good goat cheese, Gouda, sharp cheddar and a chunk of Parmesan.

Charcuterie For sandwich making or a cheese and meat tray when guests drop in, I always have the meaty essentials: salami, chorizo and prosciutto.

Ice cream Almost always you'll find good ice cream in my freezer, either the Dirty Apron homemade recipe or something from a quality local maker.

BRUNCH DISHES

This base for scones is convenient and versatile, and you can make it ahead of time. Our dried-fruit version is a traditional old-country scone. Our cheese version is a lovely moist, savoury scone. SERVES 6

Dirty Apron Scones

Basic scone mix

3⅓ c all-purpose flour

¼ c sugar

2 Tbsp + 1 tsp baking powder

1 tsp salt

⅔ c unsalted butter,
cold, cut into cubes

Dried Fruit Scones

1 egg, lightly beaten

coarse sugar, for dusting

1 recipe basic scone mix

¾ c coarsely chopped dried fruits

¾ c sour cream

¾ c milk

Spicy Cheese Scones

1 egg, lightly beaten

1 recipe basic scone mix

¾ c thick chunky salsa

¾ c milk

¾ c shredded Cheddar cheese

¼ c shredded Parmesan cheese

Basic scone mix Combine the flour, sugar, baking powder and salt in a large bowl. Using your hands, a pastry cutter or even two knives, cut in the butter until the mixture resembles coarse oatmeal. Refrigerate in an airtight container for up to 1 month or freeze for up to 3 months.

VARIATION: DRIED FRUIT SCONES

Preheat the oven to 325°F. Line a baking sheet with parchment paper. Place the egg in a shallow bowl and the sugar on a plate.

Place the scone mix in a large bowl and add the dried fruits. Pour in the sour cream and milk and mix just until the batter is moistened. Knead until a dough is formed, then press the dough into an 8-inch circle and cut into 6 equal pie-shaped wedges. Arrange the scones on the baking sheet.

Brush the scones with the beaten egg and sprinkle them with the sugar. Bake until golden, about 25 minutes. (You can test their doneness by inserting an instant-read thermometer into the dough; it should read 195°F or higher.) Remove from the oven and set on a wire rack to cool.

VARIATION: SPICY CHEESE SCONES

Preheat the oven to 325°F. Line a baking sheet with parchment paper. Place the egg in a shallow bowl.

Place the scone mix in a large bowl. Pour in the salsa, milk and cheeses and mix just until the batter is moistened. Knead until a dough is formed, then press the dough into an 8-inch circle and cut into 6 equal pie-shaped wedges. Arrange the scones on the baking sheet.

Brush the scones with the beaten egg. Bake until golden, about 25 minutes. (You can test their doneness by inserting an instant-read thermometer into the dough; it should read 195°F or higher.) Remove from the oven and set on a wire rack to cool.

CHEF'S NOTE Create your own sweet and savoury scones by mixing and matching your favourite ingredients. Just use ¾ cup total. Some of our best-sellers include white chocolate, candied ginger and lemon zest; dark chocolate, dried cranberries and orange zest; raisins and currants; unsweetened shredded coconut and dried mango; and dried figs and almonds.

If I were to open a second business, it would be a great neighbourhood breakfast spot. Breakfast is a matter of individual taste, and it's also the one meal that allows you to tap into that inner kid who wants to pour syrup over everything. Saturday and Sunday mornings at my house are a family affair, with my daughter at the kitchen island whisking the eggs, grating the Parmesan and tearing up the basil for the omelette. No matter how nicely the meal turns out, she'll always want to put ketchup on it. And that's okay—as I said, breakfast is a matter of taste.

When I think of breakfast, I think of eggs that have been poached so soft that when you break into them, the yolk forms a sauce of its own on the plate. I love double-smoked bacon and a sauce, whether it's the soft egg yolk, or a hollandaise, salsa verde or aioli. And then there's the bread. Good bread is essential to breakfast. Although you won't sit down to an elaborate breakfast most days of the week, when you do, take your time and do it right. Breakfast is a lot about multi-tasking, so learn the proper cooking times and have everything ready to come together: eggs in the pan, toast in the toaster, bacon in the oven, coffee in the grinder. There is a lovely art to breakfast, once you get it timed perfectly. If you're cooking breakfast for a big group, a little to-do sheet can help.

And the secret to a great breakfast? Think about developing the flavours and the textures for a perfect bite—eggs perfectly cooked and seasoned, paired with crisp and salty smoked bacon, crunchy toast and good maple syrup drizzled overtop. My wife tells me that in Europe they have a saying: "Eat breakfast like a king, lunch like a nobleman and dinner like a peasant." Well, this is the time to eat like a king.

BRUNCH DISHES

Make these brioches as a delicious brunch dish for guests or just as decadent sandwiches for a weekend lunch. We offer these sandwiches—an alternative to the conventional ham and cheese—on our catering menu and in the deli. The soft, rich cheese balances the saltiness of the prosciutto. YIELDS 12 BRIOCHES

Prosciutto and Taleggio Brioches

Brioche dough To make the sponge, stir together ½ c of the flour and the yeast in a large bowl. Stir in the milk until all the flour is moistened. Cover the bowl with plastic wrap and set aside in a warm place until the mixture is light and bubbly and rises and falls when you tap the bowl, about 20 minutes.

Place the sponge in the bowl of a stand mixer fitted with a hook attachment. Add the eggs and mix until well combined. Gradually add the remaining flour, sugar and salt and mix until the ingredients are moistened and evenly combined. Allow the dough to rest for 5 minutes.

With the motor running at medium speed, add ¼ of the butter and mix until fully combined. Repeat with the remaining butter, ¼ at a time. Continue mixing for about 6 minutes until the dough is uniform and it windowpanes (see Chef's Note) when stretched.

Line a baking sheet with parchment paper and lightly spray it with oil. Cut a large rectangular piece of plastic wrap and lightly spray one side with oil. Place the dough on the baking pan, form it into a 6- × 8-inch rectangle and cover tightly with the plastic wrap, oiled side down. Refrigerate the dough for at least 4 hours, preferably overnight.

Prosciutto and taleggio filling Lightly dust a work surface with flour. Place the brioche dough on the counter and roll it into a 9- × 24-inch rectangle. Generously brush egg wash evenly over the entire surface. Reserve some of the egg wash for later.

Set the brioche so that the long side is parallel to the counter. Leaving a 2-inch border along the top edge, arrange the prosciutto slices in a single layer over the entire surface. Place ½ of the taleggio in a line over the prosciutto along the bottom edge of the brioche. Holding the brioche dough at the bottom corners, gently roll the dough over the taleggio, encasing it tightly and completely. Stop rolling once you've covered the cheese. Arrange the remaining cheese in a line over the prosciutto at the base of the first roll. Continue to gently roll the brioche over the cheese and toward the top edge. You will have what looks like a large jelly roll. Cut into twelve 2-inch slices. *continued overleaf >*

Brioche dough

4 c bread flour

1 Tbsp instant yeast

½ c whole milk, warmed (90°F–95°F)

5 eggs

2½ Tbsp sugar

1½ tsp salt

2 c unsalted butter, room temperature (65°F), cut into cubes

Prosciutto and taleggio filling

2 eggs, lightly beaten

11 oz prosciutto, thinly sliced

1 lb taleggio cheese, in ½-inch slices

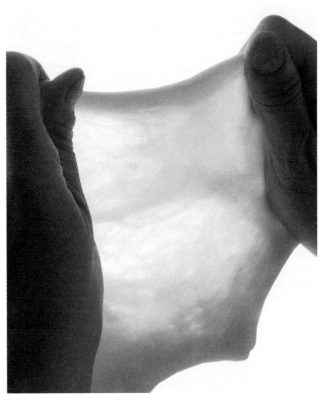
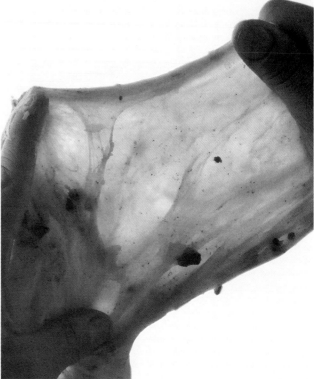

Line two baking sheets with parchment paper and lightly spray them with oil. Cut two large sheets of plastic wrap and spray them lightly on one side with oil. Arrange 6 brioches on each pan, brush them with egg wash and loosely cover them with the plastic wrap, oiled side down. Allow the brioches to proof until they have nearly doubled in size, 1 to 1½ hours.

Preheat the oven to 375°F. Bake the brioches until a thermometer inserted into the middle reads 190°F, 25 to 30 minutes. Transfer to a wire rack to cool, or serve immediately, hot from the oven.

CHEF'S NOTE Windowpaning is a way of checking that the gluten has properly formed and that your dough is emulsified. Once the dough starts to pull away from the sides of the bowl and make a slappy sound as you're mixing it, pinch off a fist-size piece. It should look shiny and feel silky smooth. Shape it into a rough rectangle, then, holding opposite sides of the rectangle in each hand, gently pull your hands apart to stretch the dough. Turn the dough 90° and stretch it again. Do this a few more times until you have a thin, translucent "windowpane." If your dough has not yet reached this stage, throw it back into the mixer and mix it for 2 minutes more.

These bagel sandwiches are simple to make and so delicious. We've elevated a classic with lemon juice and fresh dill. If you don't have salmon, use scrambled eggs instead. SERVES 6

Smoked Salmon Bagels

WITH LEMON AND DILL CREAM CHEESE

Using a fork, combine cream cheese, dill, lemon juice and black pepper in a small bowl. Season to taste, adding more lemon juice if needed.

Spread the cream cheese mixture onto the cut sides of each bagel, then top with 4 to 5 pieces of smoked salmon and garnish with watercress.

 CHEF'S NOTE   A poached egg goes nicely with this bagel.

½ c cream cheese

½ c chopped fresh dill

lemon juice, to taste

black pepper

6 sesame mini-bagels, sliced in half

8½ to 9 oz sliced smoked salmon

½ bunch of watercress, leaves only

These versatile tarts are great as an appetizer, a brunch dish or a light lunch. The peppery sharpness of the arugula contrasts nicely with the tang of the goat cheese. Make full-size tarts, or do mini versions to pass around as hors d'oeuvres. SERVES 4

Caramelized Onion and Goat Cheese Tarts

WITH ARUGULA-WALNUT PESTO

Arugula-walnut pesto

2 c loosely packed arugula leaves

2 Tbsp walnuts, toasted

2 garlic cloves, minced

2 Tbsp grated Parmesan cheese

¼ c olive oil

Caramelized onion and goat cheese tarts

1 Tbsp vegetable oil

1 large onion, thinly sliced

4 sheets of rough or classic puff pastry (pages 178 and 177), each rolled into thin, 8- × 3-inch pieces

1 egg, lightly beaten

⅓ c soft goat cheese

24 grape tomatoes, whole or sliced

¼ c walnuts, toasted

2 tsp olive oil

Arugula-walnut pesto Place the arugula, walnuts, garlic and Parmesan in a food processor and blend until the mixture is almost smooth. With the motor running, gradually add the olive oil until well blended. Season with salt and pepper.

Caramelized onion and goat cheese tarts Heat the vegetable oil in a small sauté pan over medium heat. Add the onions and, stirring constantly, cook until golden and evenly caramelized, 7 to 8 minutes. Season to taste with salt and pepper, then remove from the heat.

Preheat the oven to 425°F. While the onions are caramelizing, use the tip of a small knife to mark the puff pastry. Starting ¼ inch in from the edge of the pastry and working around all 4 sides, gently trace the outline of a rectangle. Prick the puff pastry all over with a fork, brush with egg wash and bake for 8 minutes. Leave the oven on.

Using a small knife, remove the top layers in the centre of each puff pastry (reserve for another use). Fill the centre of each puff pastry with ¼ of the goat cheese along with ¼ of the arugula-walnut pesto. Top with the onions, tomatoes and walnuts. Return the puff pastry to the oven for 2 minutes. Remove from the oven, drizzle with olive oil and serve immediately.

 CHEF'S NOTE If you don't have puff pastry handy, all of these ingredients spread on bread make an amazing sandwich.

Here's our version of a brunch classic. We've switched out the English muffin for potato, and for the hollandaise sauce, we've cut out half the butter and used extra olive oil to emulsify it. The olive oil is a nice complement to the sun-dried tomato. By the way, don't cheap out on the bacon. Use the good stuff—double-smoked only. SERVES 4

Poached Eggs on Herb Potato Rosti

WITH SUN-DRIED TOMATO HOLLANDAISE SAUCE

Herb potato rosti Preheat the oven to 180°F. Combine the potatoes, rosemary and thyme in a medium bowl and mix well. Season with salt and pepper. Using your hands, squeeze out any moisture from the potato.

Heat the vegetable oil in a nonstick pan over high heat. When the oil begins to smoke, scoop ¼ of the potato mixture into the centre of the pan, pressing it down to form an even layer that completely fills the pan. Cook until golden and crisp, 3 to 4 minutes. Reduce the heat to low. Flip the rosti over and cook until the other side is golden and crisp, 2 to 3 minutes more. Transfer the cooked rosti to a plate and place in the oven to keep warm. Repeat to make 4 rosti.

Sun-dried tomato hollandaise Melt the butter and olive oil in a small saucepan over medium heat, then remove from the heat and allow it to come to room temperature.

In a small bowl, whisk together the egg yolks, lemon juice and sun-dried tomatoes until smooth. Add the butter–olive oil mixture in a slow continuous stream, whisking constantly, until the sauce thickens. Finish with chopped parsley and season with salt and pepper. Set aside.

Poached eggs Choose a pot large enough to hold the 4 eggs at once. Fill it with 2 inches of water, add the vinegar and bring to a boil over high heat. Reduce the heat to a gentle simmer.

Have 3 or 4 paper towels on hand. Carefully crack an egg into a small bowl, then gently slide the egg into the simmering water. Repeat with the remaining eggs. Poach the eggs until the whites are completely opaque but the yolks are still soft, 3 to 4 minutes. Using a slotted spoon, transfer the eggs to a small bowl and gently blot them dry with a paper towel.

To assemble Place a rosti on each individual plate. Set two slices of bacon over the rosti, top with an egg and a few spoonfuls of the sun-dried tomato hollandaise. Serve immediately.

Herb potato rosti

2 Russet potatoes, peeled and finely julienned

2 sprigs of rosemary, chopped

2 sprigs of thyme, chopped

1 Tbsp vegetable oil

Sun-dried tomato hollandaise

⅓ c unsalted butter

¼ c olive oil

3 egg yolks

juice of 1 lemon

1½ Tbsp sun-dried tomatoes in oil, drained and finely chopped into a paste

2 sprigs of Italian parsley, finely chopped

Poached eggs

2 Tbsp white wine vinegar

4 eggs

8 slices double-smoked bacon, cooked until crisp

 CHEF'S NOTE Stay close to your pot when poaching the eggs, as they can go from soft to hard very quickly.

HOW TO POACH AN EGG

A properly poached egg is a beautiful thing, and it's worth learning how to do well because the poached egg has moved beyond the breakfast menu. In restaurants, it's showing up on salads and alongside medallions of beef. Also, a poached egg is lower in fat and healthier than an egg fried in oil. If you already have your own way of poaching eggs that works, stick with it. At the end of the day, you just want to be sure the egg keeps its shape and the white is opaque and cooked through.

Many people are intimidated by poaching eggs because they think it's more complicated than it is. It's actually pretty simple. You just need a slotted spoon, a saucepan, water, vinegar, fresh eggs and patience. And remember these tips:

1   Make sure you have the right balance of heat—if the water is too cold, the egg will fall apart; too hot, and you risk rubbery eggs. Poach at a gentle simmer because the slower you poach the egg, the better it will keep its shape.

2   Make sure you have enough water in the pot. A lot of people make the mistake of not filling the pot with enough water, and the egg ends up stuck to the bottom of the pot.

3   Use the vinegar to help stabilize the egg white, which also helps keep the egg plump. And don't worry—your egg won't have an overwhelming taste of vinegar.

4   When the egg has finished cooking, be sure to let it drain for a few seconds before plating.

If you have a lot of guests coming over, there's nothing wrong with pre-poaching eggs to a soft stage and placing them carefully into an ice bath to halt the cooking. When your guests have arrived, gently slide the eggs back into a fresh pot of hot simmering water to finish cooking for 30 to 40 seconds. When I worked at a hotel in my early days as an apprentice, we'd do eggs for 200 people in the morning, and that's how we cooked them.

If you're unsure about cooking times, here's a general guide to help:

·   Soft-poached eggs: 3–4 minutes
·   Medium-poached eggs: 4–5 minutes
·   Hard-poached eggs: 5–6 minutes

Here we use lemon zest and fresh basil, but why not substitute mint and orange zest? Or sumac? Or cinnamon? You could also switch up the basic recipe and go from sweet to savoury—crêpes are so versatile that I've made a filling with basil, fresh herbs, goat cheese and prosciutto. Sweet or savoury, I love them. Serve these crêpes with Chantilly whipped cream. SERVES 4

Lemon Basil Crêpes

WITH WARM BERRY COMPOTE

Crêpes

4 eggs

1 c all-purpose flour

3 Tbsp melted unsalted butter +
2 Tbsp, room temperature

1¾ c milk

Suggested additions

zest of 1 lemon

¼ c julienned fresh basil +
a few whole leaves for garnish

Warm berry compote

1 c fresh orange juice

2 Tbsp honey

½ vanilla bean, split lengthwise
and seeds reserved

⅔ c blueberries

⅔ c blackberries

⅔ c raspberries

2 tsp cornstarch dissolved
in 4 tsp water

Crêpes Place the eggs, flour and melted butter in a medium bowl and whisk until smooth and free of lumps. Add the milk in a thin steady stream, whisking continuously. The batter should have the consistency of cold whipping cream. Stir in the lemon zest and basil.

Heat a 9-inch nonstick or crêpe pan over medium heat. When the pan is hot, brush it with a little butter. Ladle ⅓ c of batter into the centre of the pan, then lift and tilt the pan until the batter covers the entire surface. Cook until the edges begin to brown, about 2 minutes, then flip the crêpe over to cook the other side. Transfer the cooked crêpe to a plate. Repeat with the remaining batter. (You should have about 8 crêpes.)

Warm berry compote Combine the orange juice and honey in a small saucepan over medium heat. Scrape the seeds from the vanilla bean into the saucepan, add the bean and bring to a boil, stirring to dissolve the honey, about 2 minutes. Stir in the blueberries and blackberries and cook for another minute. Gently fold in the raspberries, then stir in the cornstarch mixture and simmer gently until slightly thickened. Discard the vanilla bean and serve warm.

To serve Fold each crêpe in half, then in half again to form a pie-shaped wedge. Fold the crêpe once more and spoon the compote overtop. Serve two crêpes per person, on individual plates.

 CHEF'S NOTES Crêpes are easy to make ahead of time and freeze. Place sheets of parchment paper between the individual crêpes, then wrap them in plastic wrap. Will keep refrigerated for up to 3 days or frozen for 6 to 8 weeks.

Chantilly cream is whipped cream with a little vanilla bean to taste.

BRUNCH DISHES

Not your typical mimosa—we've spiced it up Moroccan style. We serve this sparkling juice in our brunch class at the Dirty Apron without disclosing the ingredients. Consider this the official unveiling of our secret mimosa. SERVES 4 TO 6

Moroccan Mimosas

Combine the orange juice, sumac, star anise, saffron and figs in a pitcher and refrigerate for 24 hours to allow the flavours to meld. Place a fine-mesh sieve over a large clean pitcher and strain the orange juice. Discard the solids.

Combine ⅓ of the mimosa mixture to ⅔ Cava and serve in individual champagne flutes. Enjoy!

CHEF'S NOTE A sprinkling of pretty purple sumac adds a tangy lemony flavour to meats and salads, or your mimosa. Look for it in Middle Eastern specialty stores, along with threads of yellow-orange saffron, which are reminiscent of metallic honey with grassy or hay-like notes.

2 c orange juice

1 tsp ground sumac
(see Chef's Note)

1 whole star anise

pinch of saffron (see Chef's Note)

4 to 6 dried figs

1 bottle (750 mL) Cava
sparkling wine

SOUPS AND SALADS

This rich and creamy soup is one of our deli favourites. For anyone reluctant to try squash, this soup will surely convert them. SERVES 6

Squash and Apple Soup

2 butternut squash, peeled, seeded and roughly diced

¼ c maple syrup

2 Granny Smith apples

1 Tbsp vegetable oil

3 large shallots, roughly diced

6 garlic cloves, chopped

¾ c white wine

1 c apple juice

5½ c vegetable stock (page 172)

1¼ c whipping cream

juice of 1 lemon

Preheat the oven to 450°F. Line a baking sheet with parchment paper.

Place the squash in a large bowl and season with salt and pepper. Add the maple syrup and toss until the squash is well covered. Transfer the squash to the baking sheet and roast until cooked through and slightly caramelized, about 30 minutes. Set aside.

Peel and core the apples, discarding the skins and cores, then cut the flesh into ¼-inch pieces. Set aside.

Heat the vegetable oil in a medium pot over medium heat. Add the shallots and garlic and sauté for 2 minutes. Stir in the diced apple, white wine and apple juice and cook until the liquid is reduced by half, about 10 minutes. Pour in the vegetable stock and bring to a boil, then add the roasted squash, including the cooking juices. Add the cream, reduce the heat to a simmer and cook for about 10 minutes. Remove from the heat.

Using a hand blender, purée the soup until smooth. Stir in the lemon juice and season to taste with salt and pepper.

CHEF'S NOTE It's always a good idea to have some extra vegetable stock on hand, in case you need to slightly thin the soup.

This is another rich, delicious soup, and, with all the dicing, a great way to practise your knife skills. And here's a little tip: buy shallots instead of onions. They're smaller, so you get the rich flavour of onions without wondering what to do with an unused half onion left sitting in your fridge. SERVES 4 TO 6

Grilled Corn and Clam Chowder

Heat the white wine in a small saucepan over medium-high heat. Add the clams, cover and steam with the lid on until all the clams have opened, about 5 minutes. Remove from the heat.

Discard any clams that have not opened. Using a slotted spoon, transfer the clams to a bowl. Separate the meat from the shells, discarding the shells and reserving both the clam meat and any clam juices. Set aside.

Line a plate with paper towels. Place the bacon in a small saucepan and sauté over medium heat until brown and crisp, about 6 minutes. Using a slotted spoon, transfer the bacon to the paper towel–lined plate.

Pour off and discard all but 1 Tbsp of the bacon fat. Add the shallots, carrots and garlic and sauté over medium-low heat for 2 to 3 minutes. Stir in the potatoes, clam nectar and reserved clam juices and bring to a boil. Reduce the heat to low and simmer until the vegetables are tender, about 10 minutes.

While the soup is simmering, preheat a grill to high heat. Place the corn on the grill, turning the cobs often to cook all sides until tender and charred, 6 to 7 minutes total. Remove from the heat and set aside until cool enough to handle. Using a sharp knife, cut the kernels off the cob into a small bowl and set aside. Discard the cobs.

To the simmering soup, add the cream, reserved clam meat, lemon juice, corn, thyme and bacon. Increase the heat to high, bring the soup back to a boil and add the cornstarch mixture, stirring constantly until the soup reaches your desired consistency. Remove from the heat and season to taste with salt and pepper.

Ladle the chowder into individual bowls and garnish with the chives.

1 c white wine

30 fresh clams
(we use Manila clams)

8 oz double-smoked bacon,
in ½-inch dice

3 shallots, diced

½ carrot, diced

2 garlic cloves, minced

½ lb red potatoes, unpeeled
but cut in small dice

2 c clam nectar (see Chef's Note)

2 ears fresh corn, shucked

2 c whipping cream

2 Tbsp lemon juice

2 tsp chopped fresh thyme

2 tsp cornstarch mixed
with 1 Tbsp cold water

2 tsp finely sliced chives
(optional)

CHEF'S NOTES Clam nectar is a broth from clams, sold in small bottles or cans in the soup aisle of most grocery stores.

Taste this soup carefully before seasoning it with salt, as a lot of the ingredients used in this soup are naturally salty.

This dish is close to my heart. It was one of the first soups I ever made as a young apprentice, and I still make it regularly for the deli and at home. SERVES 4 TO 6

Porcini Mushroom and Chestnut Soup

½ Tbsp vegetable oil

1 small onion, diced

2 garlic cloves, minced

1 oz dried porcini mushrooms, soaked in water, drained and sliced

1 Russet potato, peeled and diced

1 lb chestnuts, peeled

6 c vegetable stock (page 172)

1 c whipping cream

1 Tbsp olive oil

2 oz fresh porcini mushrooms, cut into 1-inch pieces

1 Tbsp sherry vinegar

2 sprigs of fresh thyme, leaves only

truffle oil to taste

Heat the vegetable oil in a large saucepan over medium-high heat. Add the onions, half the garlic and the dried mushrooms and sauté until the onions are soft, 3 to 4 minutes. Add the potatoes and chestnuts and sauté for a few more minutes. Reduce the heat to medium, pour in the vegetable stock and cream, and simmer until the potatoes and chestnuts are soft, about 8 minutes. Remove from the heat.

Using a hand blender or food processor, purée the soup until smooth. Season with salt and pepper. Return the soup to low heat to keep warm.

Heat the olive oil in a sauté pan over medium heat. Add the fresh mushrooms and the remaining garlic and sauté until tender and golden, 3 to 4 minutes. Deglaze the pan with sherry vinegar.

Ladle the hot soup into individual bowls and garnish with the sautéed mushrooms and thyme leaves. Drizzle the mushrooms with truffle oil.

 CHEF'S NOTE If you don't have fresh porcini mushrooms on hand, portobello or button mushrooms are good substitutes.

A classic hearty Tuscan soup filled with beans, ham and vegetables, the ribollita has become a favourite with our customers. Turn it into a vegetarian dish just by omitting the meat and using vegetable stock: either way, you'll be wanting seconds. SERVES 6

Ribollita Soup

Heat the olive oil in a large pot over medium-low heat. Stir in the onions and sauté for 5 minutes until they begin to sweat. Add the garlic, bay leaves, cinnamon stick, fennel seeds, coriander seeds, cumin seeds, chili flakes and ham and cook for 5 to 6 minutes. Stir in the carrots, celery, tomato sauce and stock; increase the heat to medium and allow to come to a boil. Reduce the heat to low and simmer for 30 minutes. Season with salt and pepper and add the lemon juice, kale and navy beans. Serve hot!

 CHEF'S NOTE You can substitute bacon, pancetta or prosciutto for the ham.

1 Tbsp olive oil

2 white onions, peeled and cut in medium dice

6 garlic cloves, minced

6 bay leaves

1 cinnamon stick

2 Tbsp fennel seeds

2 Tbsp coriander seeds

2 Tbsp cumin seeds

pinch of chili flakes

2 c diced ham

2 carrots, peeled and cut in medium dice

2 celery stalks, cut in medium dice

1 can (15 oz) tomato sauce

4 c chicken or beef stock (page 173)

¼ c lemon juice

1 bunch of kale, stems removed, chopped

2 c cooked white navy beans

Do not underestimate the power of a really good soup. We go through six to seven gallons of soup a day at the Dirty Apron because our customers love good soup. And soup always tastes better the next day, so if you're planning a dinner party, make the soup the day before. There is nothing inferior about leftover soup. If I had my way, the expression would be *soupe du next day*, not *soupe du jour*.

A great soup always starts with a great stock—it's what brings the whole soup together. Aside from a vegetable stock, all my stocks start with bones, including chicken, meat or fish bones. When I'm cooking, I always have a future stock in mind, which means I am constantly putting aside the bits and scraps that will be the flavour enhancers of my stock. I put onion peels, carrot peels, garlic peels, celery ends, and the like in a plastic bag or container that I keep in the fridge. This flavour base, called a *mirepoix* in cooking school, is not a garbage bin, so you have to think about what you're adding to it. For example, root vegetables have a lot of starch and can make the stock turn cloudy. Also, lemon and other acidic ingredients that become bitter with cooking are not good for a stock. Generally try to scrape together a pound of mirepoix for every sixteen cups of stock.

My rule when making the soup itself is taste, taste, taste, and taste again. All good cooks develop a sophisticated palate by tasting and adjusting, repeatedly. Have you got the right amount of seasoning? My advice is to go easy on the salt at the beginning because as the soup cooks, it reduces and the salt will intensify. (Salt can be your best friend or your worst enemy when making soup.) Have you got a bit of acidity? There's nothing wrong with a splash of citrus or vinegar to bring out the other flavours. Do you need some dried spices to elevate the flavour profile? Start with a pinch. And once you've got the seasoning just where you want it, know that it will be even more delicious the next day.

Inspired by my trips to Southeast Asia, this salad can be served with anything—it's that good. Shiso leaf is basically Japan's version of mint, and it adds another dimension to the succulent sweetness of the mango. The salad is great on its own, served with fish or meat, or in a sandwich. SERVES 4

Mango Salad

1 Tbsp brown or palm sugar

2 Tbsp lime juice

1 Tbsp soy sauce

½ tsp crushed chilies or to taste

2 large ripe mangoes, peeled and cut into thin strips

½ c thinly sliced red onions

1 c bean sprouts

3 shiso leaves, julienned

3 sprigs of Thai basil, leaves only

In a bowl, mix together the sugar, lime juice, soy sauce and chilies. Fold in the mango, onions, bean sprouts, shiso leaves and Thai basil. Season with salt and pepper. Serve immediately.

CHEF'S NOTES If you like spicy food, use the full amount of chilies. Otherwise, start with ¼ tsp, taste and add more as needed.

Papaya is a great substitute for the mango.

The beet might be a restaurant trend, but it's not going anywhere.
And this beet and citrus salad is a summer classic. SERVES 6

Golden Beet Salad

Place the beets in a large pot, cover with water and boil until fork-tender, 30 to 45 minutes. Drain the beets, then peel and quarter each one. Set aside.

Peel the oranges and grapefruits. Working over a medium bowl and using a sharp knife, run the blade under the skins surrounding each segment to release the flesh, catching any escaping juice. Discard the peels and skins, reserving the orange and grapefruit segments and their juice in the bowl. Add the beets, radicchio, watercress, olives and maple syrup. Toss gently and arrange on a serving plate. Drizzle olive oil on top, garnish with the chives and enjoy this refreshing salad!

 —————
CHEF'S NOTE To save time, it is okay to prepare your beets a day or two in advance.

6 large golden beets

3 oranges

3 grapefruits

1 head of radicchio, separated into leaves and gently torn

2 bunches of watercress, leaves only

½ c kalamata olives, pitted

¼ c maple syrup

¼ c olive oil

6 chives, thinly sliced

Cutting the vegetables in different sizes and styles adds to
the stunning visual presentation of this dish. SERVES 6

Roasted Root Vegetable Salad

3 large carrots, peeled

3 large parsnips, peeled

2 sweet potatoes, peeled

2 yams, peeled

½ c olive oil, plus ¼ c for drizzling

⅓ c sherry vinegar

2 Tbsp Dijon mustard

⅓ c maple syrup

⅓ c capers

2 bunches of watercress, torn into pieces

2 pints confit tomatoes (page 172)

Preheat the oven to 450°F. Cut the carrots and parsnips into matchsticks about ¼ inch wide and ½ inch long. Do not be exact: the idea is to have them all slightly different sizes. Then cut the sweet potatoes and yams into a range of bite-size triangles. Arrange each vegetable in a single layer in a separate roasting pan, drizzle with olive oil and season with salt and pepper. Toss lightly so the vegetables are well coated with the oil. Bake for 15 to 20 minutes until the vegetables are cooked through and have a bit of colour. (The vegetables will cook at different rates since they have been cut to different sizes. Watch them carefully so you don't burn or overcook them.) Set aside to cool. Reduce the oven temperature to 350°F.

In a small bowl, combine the sherry vinegar, Dijon mustard and maple syrup. Slowly whisk in the ½ cup of olive oil until emulsified. Season with salt and pepper, then add the capers.

In a large bowl, toss together the root vegetables and enough dressing to generously coat them. Transfer to a serving plate and garnish with watercress and confit tomatoes.

CHEF'S NOTE Cook each of the vegetables separately, as each vegetable has a different cooking time. This will ensure every vegetable is cooked to perfection!

Many of us grew up eating steamed broccoli and cauliflower and consider these vegetables super boring. But the simple addition of chorizo elevates them to a whole other flavour profile. This dish is excellent served hot or cold. SERVES 6

Chorizo, Broccoli and Cauliflower Salad

Heat the olive oil over medium-high heat. Add the onions, season with salt and pepper and sauté for 1 to 2 minutes. Stir in the chorizo and garlic and cook for about a minute. Toss in the cauliflower, cook for a minute and then add the broccoli and sauté for 2 minutes more. The vegetables in this dish should stay rather firm, so be sure not to overcook them. Pour in sherry vinegar and a dash of olive oil. Serve immediately or set aside to cool.

CHEF'S NOTE Drizzling olive oil over the top of the salad is a nice touch, as is garnishing it with parsley or other fresh herbs.

1 Tbsp olive oil, plus more for drizzling

2 red onions, sliced

2 fresh chorizo sausages, in 1-inch dice

3 garlic cloves, minced

1 head of cauliflower, florets only

1 bunch of broccoli, florets only

dash of sherry vinegar

KALE AND OTHER TRENDS

I'm fascinated with how food evolves and how quickly, as a culture, our collective palates have broadened. Some trends make sense; others have limited appeal. For example, molecular gastronomy taps the potential of food as science and art, but it will always remain in the domain of the trained professional simply because the average home kitchen isn't stocked with xanthan gum and alginates.

But I welcome food trends because they indicate how far we've come in our level of knowledge of and our interest in food. What we eat is playing a bigger role in our lives than ever before, and we're taking it far more seriously. We read labels, books and news reports on food. We follow cooking shows. We look upon certain cooks as celebrities. We realize that our day-to-day food choices shape our health. And perhaps, in a world where everything has become more chain-store generic and globalized, we want to know where our food is coming from.

We now take more interest in whether our lamb is from New Zealand or Salt Spring Island and what makes a chanterelle different from an oyster mushroom. We are less wasteful and more open-minded. We prize foods we used to turn up our noses at: sablefish for its omega-3 fatty acids, for example, or short rib for its affordability and flavour. These days, it's a testament to the chef's skill to use every device in the toolbox to showcase these harder-to-cook ingredients. We also want to buy quality products and support the mom-and-pop restaurateurs, butchers, growers and cheese artisans, because we want fresh, locally sourced food. That's one food trend I can definitely get behind.

These days, the whole world loves kale. At the Dirty Apron, a dish with kale outsells everything else five to one. In this dish, the crisp kale holds its own against the acidity of a traditional Caesar dressing. SERVES 6

Kale Caesar Salad

Caesar dressing In a food processor, blend together the egg yolks, anchovies, garlic, Dijon mustard and vinegar until smooth. Slowly drizzle in the canola oil until emulsified. The dressing should look thick and creamy. Season to taste with salt, pepper and lemon juice. Will keep refrigerated in an airtight container for up to 2 weeks.

Croutons Preheat the oven to 375°F. Place the bread in a large bowl. Add the garlic, oregano, thyme and ¼ cup of the olive oil and season with salt and pepper. Toss, adding more olive oil as necessary, until the bread is nicely saturated with the olive oil. Arrange the bread in a single layer on a baking sheet and bake for 5 to 7 minutes, or until golden. Shake the baking sheet to loosen the croutons and set aside to cool.

Kale salad Bring a large pot of water to a boil on high heat. Gently drop in the eggs and cook for 10 minutes. While the eggs are cooking, fill a large bowl with ice water. Transfer the cooked eggs to the ice water to cool quickly. When the eggs are cool enough to handle, peel them, discarding the shells, and cut the eggs into quarters. Set aside.

In a bowl, toss together the kale with the Caesar dressing, until all the leaves are coated. Add the croutons and boiled eggs, then garnish with shaved Parmesan. Serve immediately.

 CHEF'S NOTE Any variety of kale will work. We like to use a mixture of different seasonal varieties for colour contrast and texture!

Caesar dressing

3 egg yolks

3 anchovy fillets

5 garlic cloves, peeled

3 Tbsp Dijon mustard

¼ c red wine vinegar or sherry vinegar

1 c canola oil

2 Tbsp lemon juice

Croutons

1 day-old French baguette or sourdough bread, in 1-inch dice

3 garlic cloves, minced

3 Tbsp dried oregano

2 Tbsp dried thyme

⅓ c olive oil

Kale salad

4 eggs

3 to 4 bunches of kale, washed, stems removed and leaves cut into bite-size pieces

¼ c shaved Parmesan cheese

The name of this dish says it all. The subtle sweetness of the confit tomatoes and caramelized fennel, the tartness of the cheese and the salty crispiness of the pancetta are a delicious blend. Serve this salad hot or cold on its own, or as a side dish to any protein. SERVES 6

Caramelized Fennel and Goat Cheese Salad

WITH PANCETTA CRISPS AND CONFIT CHERRY TOMATOES

4 heads of fennel, stems removed

½ c maple syrup

¼ c sherry vinegar

3 Tbsp olive oil

1 c pancetta, in paper-thin slices

2 tsp brown sugar

2 bunches of watercress, torn into pieces

20 confit tomatoes (page 172)

1 c crumbled goat cheese

Preheat the oven to 450°F. Slice the fennel into 1-inch-thick pieces and arrange in a single layer in a roasting pan. Drizzle with maple syrup, sherry vinegar and olive oil. Season with salt and pepper and toss lightly until the fennel is evenly coated. Bake for 15 minutes, or until the fennel is golden and caramelized. Set aside. Reduce the oven temperature to 350°F.

Line a baking sheet with parchment paper. Arrange the pancetta on the baking sheet, sprinkle evenly with the brown sugar and bake for 4 to 7 minutes or until crisp. Set aside.

To assemble the salad, layer the watercress and fennel on a plate, then garnish with confit tomatoes, pancetta and goat cheese. Enjoy!

 CHEF'S NOTE Save the olive oil from the confit tomatoes to confit other foods, or use it in salad dressings or drizzle it over finished dishes as you would other flavoured oils.

ENGLISH

DELI LUNCHES

When the Dirty Apron deli first opened, the popularity of this sandwich helped spread the word. We roast chickens every day for this sandwich, and the garlic, lemon and thyme flavours marry beautifully with the chipotle mayonnaise. SERVES 6

Roast Chicken Sandwich

Roast chicken sandwiches

1 whole chicken, 2½ to 3 lbs

1 head of garlic, cut in half

1 bunch of fresh thyme

2 lemons, sliced in half

olive oil, as needed

3 French baguettes

½ c shaved Parmesan cheese

½ c sun-dried tomatoes in oil, drained and sliced

1 bunch of watercress, in sprigs

Chipotle mayonnaise

½ c mayonnaise

2 Tbsp chipotle chilies in adobo

Roast chicken sandwiches Preheat the oven to 375°F. Rinse the chicken inside and out and pat dry with a paper towel. Stuff the cavity with garlic, thyme and lemons and place the chicken in a roasting pan. Season with salt and pepper, drizzle with olive oil and bake for 45 to 60 minutes. Insert the tip of a sharp knife in the meatiest part and if the juices run clear, the chicken is ready. Remove from the oven and allow it to cool.

Using your hands, pull the chicken meat from the bones, making sure not to get any bones or skin mixed in with the meat. Save the skin and bones for stock.

Chipotle mayonnaise Combine the mayonnaise and chipotle in a small bowl.

Finish sandwiches Cut each baguette in half widthwise. Slice each half lengthwise without cutting all the way through the baguette. Press open the bread.

Spread chipotle mayonnaise on each side of the open baguette, then top with Parmesan cheese, sun-dried tomatoes, chicken and watercress. Dig in!

This lamb dish has a Moroccan theme going on. What's great is that it can be a stew one day, a sandwich the next. Start the lamb and the pickled onions the day before you plan to serve this sandwich so they have time to marinate. Prepare the spiced yoghurt and the chickpeas while the meat is cooking. SERVES 6

Braised Lamb Sandwich

WITH SPICED YOGHURT

Braised lamb sandwiches

1 Tbsp olive oil

3 white onions, diced

2 heads of garlic, smashed

½ c diced fresh ginger

3 Tbsp cumin seeds

3 Tbsp coriander seeds

3 Tbsp turmeric

1 Tbsp chili flakes

2 Tbsp mustard seeds

2 cinnamon sticks

10 bay leaves

3 Tbsp salt

2 Tbsp black pepper

1 bottle (750 mL) dry white wine

4 c chicken stock (page 173)

1 c + 2 Tbsp honey

1 lamb shoulder, 4½ lbs

1 loaf of raisin brioche,
sliced and toasted

1 bunch of cilantro, roughly torn

Pickled red onions

½ c red wine vinegar

⅓ c sugar

1 large red onion, thinly
sliced on a mandolin

Braised lamb sandwiches Heat the olive oil in a large pot over medium heat. Add the onions, garlic, ginger, cumin seeds, coriander seeds, turmeric, chili flakes, mustard seeds, cinnamon sticks, bay leaves, salt and black pepper and sauté for 7 to 10 minutes. Pour in the white wine, then bring to a boil. Add the chicken stock and bring back to a boil. Add 1 cup of the honey, then reduce the heat to low and simmer for 30 minutes. Allow this braising liquid to cool completely.

While the liquid is cooling, season the lamb with salt and pepper. Heat a frying pan on high heat until hot. Add the lamb and sear on all sides until the meat is a deep gold, about 10 minutes total. Pour the cooled liquid into a baking pan, add the lamb and refrigerate, covered, for 24 hours.

Pickled red onions Have ready an 8 oz canning jar with a sealable lid. Bring a large pot of water to a boil over high heat. Using tongs, place the jar, lid and sealing band into the boiling water and allow to sit for 2 minutes. Transfer the sterilized jar and lid pieces to a tea towel or dish rack to drain.

Place the vinegar in a small saucepan over medium heat. Add the sugar and heat, stirring, until dissolved. Do not allow to boil. Once the sugar has dissolved, remove from the heat and allow to cool completely.

Place the onions in the sterilized glass jar, cover with the cold sweetened vinegar, seal tightly and refrigerate for at least 24 hours. Will keep refrigerated for up to 3 months.

Finish braised lamb Preheat the oven to 350°F. Cook the lamb in its braising liquid, covered, for 5 to 6 hours, until the meat is completely tender. Remove from the oven and allow to rest for 1 hour. Drain off the braising liquid and save as a base for soup or curry.

Spiced yoghurt Combine all the ingredients in a bowl. Will keep refrigerated in an airtight container for up to 7 days.

Fried chickpeas Line a plate with paper towels. Heat the canola oil in a large deep-sided pot over medium heat until it reaches 375°F. (Drop a chickpea into the hot oil; if it sizzles, it's ready.)

    Carefully add the chickpeas to the oil and fry until golden and crispy, about 5 minutes. Using a slotted spoon, transfer the chickpeas to the paper towel–lined plate.

Finish sandwiches Using your fingers, pull the warm braised lamb from the bone in bite-size pieces.

    Spread one side of each brioche slice with some of the spiced yoghurt. For each sandwich, top one piece of bread with pickled red onions, cilantro, fried chickpeas and a generous pile of lamb. Drizzle with honey and top with the second slice of bread. Serve warm, with lots of napkins at hand.

Spiced yoghurt

½ c plain Greek yoghurt

1 preserved lemon, peel only, minced

3 garlic cloves, minced

2 Tbsp dried mint

2 Tbsp lemon juice

1 cucumber, grated with a cheese grater

Fried chickpeas

3 c canola oil

½ c cooked chickpeas

People often ask me what I like to eat when I'm not being a chef, and my answer is always the same: a sandwich. Since I was a kid, I have loved making sandwiches, and I think they're the reason I became a chef. They're an easy place to start because there's no oven required.

When I was seven years old, I thought it was creative genius to slather white bread with mayonnaise and a sprinkling of chocolate chips. Thankfully, my palate has become a little more refined. My mother, a great home cook, made delicious soups and sandwiches for weekend lunches, and she taught me that there's an art to making a great sandwich. You have to know your flavours, they have to work together and you want an essential balance of fresh, sweet, salty, tart, crispy and fatty.

To create your own killer sandwich, start with a few of our recipes here and feel free to improvise to make them your very own. That's what sandwich making is all about.

Of course, a great sandwich starts with great bread. At the Dirty Apron, we've gone through umpteen varieties of bread to determine the perfect one for our sandwiches. Good sandwich bread needs a crisp crust, and it has to be able to hold the ingredients without getting soggy or falling apart. The filling ingredients must be fresh and high quality: you should have a saltiness from meat, cheese or pickles; a freshness from herbs or vegetables; and a layer of fat like a mayonnaise or olive oil or aioli. Those are the keys to a memorable sandwich.

At the Dirty Apron, we follow these rules and we've garnered a loyal lunchtime following. But I've discovered that sandwiches are an intensely individual choice. We have a customer who's been coming in for three years, Monday through Friday, and he always orders the crab and shrimp. Another guy orders the roast chicken every time. Another comes in for the lamb. These preferences are so established that our sandwich menu can't change, or we lose customers. What this means is that every new sandwich goes through several rounds of testing among the team. Before we put it on the menu, we want to be absolutely sure that it's going to be a winner with our customers.

To make our Dirty Apron version of the classic Vietnamese bánh mì sandwich, we braise the pork in spices for six hours so that it's juicy and packed with intense flavour. The pickled daikon and carrot give this sandwich crunch, and the kick from the sambal adds yet another layer of flavour. Start the pickled vegetables the day before you plan to serve this sandwich. SERVES 6

Vietnamese-Style Pulled Pork Baguette

Pulled pork baguettes

½ c chopped fresh ginger

2 Tbsp coriander seeds

pinch of cloves

½ c chipotle chilies in adobo

1 can (28 oz) tomato sauce

½ c tomato paste

3 large white onions, diced

1 c chopped garlic

4 c soy sauce

4 c balsamic vinegar

4 oranges, sliced

2 Tbsp salt

1 c brown sugar

1 pork butt, 4 to 5 lbs

1 c cornstarch mixed with ⅓ c water

3 French baguettes

3 Tbsp spicy mustard (see below)

sprigs of fresh cilantro

Pickled vegetables

⅓ c red wine vinegar

⅓ c sugar

2 carrots, peeled and julienned

1 daikon, peeled and julienned

Spicy mustard

2 onions, caramelized (page 72)

1 c grainy Dijon mustard

2 Tbsp sherry vinegar

Pulled pork baguettes Using your hands, combine the ginger, coriander seeds, cloves, chipotle, tomato sauce, tomato paste, onions, garlic, soy sauce, balsamic vinegar, oranges, salt and brown sugar in a large ovenproof pot. Really get in there and mix the ingredients together. Add the pork butt and refrigerate, covered, for at least 12 hours or up to 3 days.

Pickled vegetables Have ready an 8 oz canning jar with a sealable lid. Bring a large pot of water to a boil over high heat. Using tongs, place the jar, lid and sealing band into the boiling water and allow to sit for 2 minutes. Transfer the sterilized jar and lid pieces to a tea towel or dish rack to drain.

Place the vinegar in a small saucepan over medium heat. Add the sugar, and heat, stirring, until dissolved. Do not allow to boil. Once the sugar has dissolved, remove from the heat and allow to cool completely.

Place the carrots and daikon in the sterilized glass jar, cover with the cold sweetened vinegar, seal tightly and refrigerate for at least 24 hours. Will keep refrigerated for up to 3 months.

Finish pulled pork Preheat the oven to 350°F. Make sure the pork is submerged in the liquid, cover the pan with aluminum foil and cook for 5 to 6 hours, or until the meat is tender and easily pulls away from itself. Remove from the oven and allow the pork to cool completely in the braising liquid.

Remove the pork from the liquid and, using a fork or your fingers, pull the pork into long bite-size pieces. Set aside.

Place a fine-mesh sieve over a small clean saucepan. Strain the braising liquid through the sieve and discard the solids. Place the saucepan of strained liquid over medium heat, whisk in the cornstarch mixture and bring to a boil. It will thicken, and you will have a BBQ sauce to pour over the finished sandwich. Set aside.

Spicy mustard Combine onions, Dijon mustard and vinegar in a food processor until smooth. Will keep refrigerated in an airtight container for up to 1 month.

Sambal mayonnaise Combine the mayonnaise and sambal in a small bowl.

Finish sandwiches Add the pulled pork to the BBQ sauce and warm gently in a small pot over medium heat.

    Cut each baguette in half widthwise. Slice each half lengthwise without cutting all the way through the baguette. Press open the bread. Spread the sambal mayonnaise and spicy mustard on each side of the open baguette, then top with pulled pork. Garnish with pickled vegetables and fresh cilantro. Serve with a dollop of BBQ sauce and a heap of napkins.

Sambal mayonnaise

½ c mayonnaise

2 Tbsp sambal oelek
(hot chili sauce)

This flatbread is astonishingly easy to make, so don't be intimidated. The result is a thin, softly textured bread that can double as a wrap, but bake it for longer and it will crisp up nicely for use as a pizza crust. As a flatbread, serve it alongside Thai food or topped with deli items, like goat cheese and prosciutto, or make an appetizer platter with these three dips. SERVES 4

Flatbread

WITH TOMATO-WALNUT SALSA, BABA GANOUSH AND HUMMUS

Tomato-walnut salsa

1 red onion, roughly diced

2 red bell peppers, roughly diced

5 Roma tomatoes, roughly diced

1 jalapeño pepper,
seeded and roughly diced

½ bunch of cilantro

½ c walnuts, toasted

4 Tbsp olive oil

4 Tbsp pomegranate molasses
(see Chef's Note)

2 Tbsp lemon juice

Baba ganoush

1 large purple eggplant

¼ c olive oil

1 tsp cumin seeds,
toasted and ground

¼ c plain yoghurt

juice of 1 lemon

2 garlic cloves, peeled

Hummus

2 c dried chickpeas

½ tsp salt + 1 Tbsp for boiling

½ c olive oil

¼ c tahini (see Chef's Note)

1 Tbsp ground cumin

1 garlic clove, peeled

½ tsp chili flakes

⅓ c lemon juice

1 tsp dry mint

Tomato-walnut salsa Place the onions, bell peppers, tomatoes, jalapeño peppers, cilantro and walnuts in a food processor and pulse until the vegetables are small enough to fit on a chip! Transfer to a large bowl and season with salt, pepper, olive oil, pomegranate molasses and lemon juice. Will keep refrigerated in an airtight container for up to 10 days. Makes 3 cups.

Baba ganoush Preheat the oven to 400°F. Line a baking sheet with parchment paper. Roughly peel and cut up the eggplant—there is no need to be fancy, as the eggplant will be blended later. Place the eggplant in a bowl with ⅛ cup of the olive oil, cumin seeds and a little salt and pepper. Arrange the eggplant in a single layer on the baking sheet and bake for at least 20 minutes, until the eggplant is very dark and looks almost burnt. Remove from the oven and allow it to cool.

In a food processor, blend together the eggplant, yoghurt, lemon juice and garlic until smooth. With the motor running, slowly incorporate the remaining ⅛ cup of olive oil until well mixed. Season to taste with salt and pepper. Will keep refrigerated in an airtight container for up to 10 days. Makes 1 cup.

Hummus Place the chickpeas in a large bowl, cover them with water and allow them to soak overnight. Drain the chickpeas and transfer them to a large pot. Cover the chickpeas with cold water, add the 1 Tbsp of salt and cook over medium heat until soft, about 1½ hours. Drain the chickpeas, reserving 1 cup of the cooking liquid.

Place the chickpeas and cooking liquid in a food processor along with the remaining ingredients. Blend until smooth. Season to taste with a little more lemon juice. Will keep refrigerated in an airtight container for up to 10 days. Makes 4 cups.

Flatbreads Mix the water and yeast in a medium bowl and allow to stand for 5 minutes. Add 2 Tbsp of the olive oil, the flour and the salt and stir until all the ingredients are combined.

Lightly dust a work surface with flour. Lightly coat a large bowl with 1 Tbsp of the olive oil. Turn the dough out onto the counter and knead until smooth, 3 to 4 minutes. Place the dough in the oiled bowl and turn it until well coated. Cover with a damp cloth and set aside in a warm place until the dough has doubled in size, about 1 hour.

Heat the grill to high. Also preheat the oven to 425°F. Lightly dust a work surface with flour. Gently press on the dough to release some of the air, then transfer it to the counter. Divide the dough into two equal pieces and roll out each one until it is flat and about 1½ inches thick. Brush the top with olive oil, place the flatbreads oiled side down on the grill and cook until golden and lightly charred, about 1 minute. Brush the top side of the flatbreads with more olive oil, turn them over and continue grilling until the bottoms are golden, about 1 minute. For crispier flatbread, place the grilled breads on a baking sheet and bake in the oven for 5 minutes.

Place salsa, baba ganoush and/or hummus in individual bowls. Serve flatbreads warm from the oven or at room temperature with the spreads alongside.

 CHEF'S NOTES This flatbread goes well on its own, but works very well as an accompaniment to curries, stews and soups.

Seek out the thick, fragrant and tangy reduction of pomegranate molasses and the tahini sesame seed paste in Middle Eastern food stores.

Flatbreads

¾ c warm water (105°F–115°F)

1 tsp active dry yeast

6 Tbsp olive oil

2 c all-purpose flour + more for rolling

1 tsp salt

This quick and simple dish is fantastic served hot or cold. Whip it up one night and serve the leftovers for lunch the next day. Your kids will love it too. SERVES 4

Tomato and Lemon Orzo Pasta

Bring a large pot of salted water to a boil over high heat. Add the orzo and cook for 8 to 10 minutes, or until al dente. Drain the orzo, transfer to a serving bowl and toss with the olive oil.

In a small bowl, combine the garlic, tomatoes, lemon juice and lemon zest, and the parsley. Pour this mixture over the pasta and toss together until combined. Season to taste with salt and pepper. Serve hot or cold.

1 c orzo

¼ c olive oil

2 garlic cloves, minced

16 cherry tomatoes, cut in half

juice and zest of 2 lemons

¼ c chopped parsley

 CHEF'S NOTE Feel free to use a different type of small pasta such as penne or even couscous if you don't have orzo on hand.

Ricotta replaces the usual potato in this gnocchi, and, as a result, this dish takes a tenth of the time to make. In Italy, it's common to see ricotta gnocchi like this made with fresh herbs. These gnocchi can be served right after boiling, sautéed in butter until golden and sprinkled with chopped fresh herbs, or reheated in a sauce. SERVES 4

Herb Ricotta Gnocchi
WITH CHANTERELLE CREAM SAUCE

Herb ricotta gnocchi

1 c ricotta cheese

¼ c finely grated
Parmesan cheese

1 Tbsp olive oil

1 Tbsp finely chopped
Italian parsley

⅓ c all-purpose flour +
more for rolling

Chanterelle cream sauce

½ Tbsp olive oil

2 shallots, finely diced

2 garlic cloves, minced

3 c chanterelle mushrooms

⅔ c red wine

¾ c beef stock (page 173)

⅓ c whipping cream

2 Tbsp grated Parmesan cheese

2 tsp cornstarch mixed
with 4 tsp cold water

16 asparagus spears, trimmed
and cut into 1-inch pieces

Herb ricotta gnocchi Place the ricotta cheese in a fine-mesh strainer set over a bowl for about half an hour. Pour off any extra liquid.

Combine the ricotta, Parmesan cheese, olive oil and parsley until well mixed, then season with salt and pepper. Gently mix in the flour by hand until the mixture has formed a dough.

Lightly dust a baking sheet and a work surface with flour. Lightly coat a second baking sheet with oil.

Dust the dough with flour, then using your hands, roll it into a rope about ¾ inch in diameter. Using a sharp knife, cut the rope into 1-inch pieces and place them on the floured baking sheet.

Bring a large pot of water to a boil over high heat. Drop the gnocchi into the water and cook until they float to the surface, about 1 minute. Using a slotted spoon, transfer them to the oiled baking sheet to keep them from sticking to each other. Allow the gnocchi to cool.

Chanterelle cream sauce Heat a medium saucepan over medium heat. Add the olive oil, shallots and garlic and cook until tender, about 2 minutes. Add the chanterelles and sauté for about 1 minute. Pour in the red wine and bring to a boil; then add the beef stock and reduce the mixture by a third, 6 to 7 minutes. Stir in the cream and continue to simmer for another minute.

While the sauce is simmering, stir in the Parmesan and the cornstarch mixture. Once the sauce has thickened slightly, add the gnocchi and asparagus and simmer for another minute. Serve immediately.

CHEF'S NOTES Keep in mind that this gnocchi mixture is very versatile. You can always add other fresh herbs and dried spices to the parsley (or replace it entirely) to create different flavours.

Take the time to sauté the shallots, garlic and mushrooms properly, as they will develop a great flavour foundation for the sauce.

This ravioli is a classroom favourite at the Dirty Apron—even the hardcore carnivores love it. Make a big batch of ravioli and freeze it for future use or serve it as a vegetarian main course. SERVES 4

Arugula and Goat Cheese Ravioli

WITH WALNUT AND SAGE BUTTER SAUCE

Arugula and goat cheese ravioli Finely chop the arugula and place it in a small bowl. Add the olive oil and the cheeses, combine well, and season with salt and pepper.

Lightly dust a work surface with flour. Cut a sheet of pasta in half and arrange it with the long side parallel to the counter. Fill a small bowl with cold water.

Using a tablespoon, mound a bit of the filling in the centre of the pasta sheet about an inch in from one end. Mound the next bit of filling about 2 inches from the first one. Continue until the sheet is covered with spoonfuls of filling. Remember to leave about an inch between the last bit of filling and the far edge of the pasta. Dip your finger in the cold water and lightly brush the pasta in between the fillings. Place the other half of the pasta sheet over the mounds of the fillings. Gently press in between the mounds to seal the filling in and press any air out. Using a ravioli cutter (or a round cutter or a sharp knife), cut the pasta into squares or circles. Repeat with the remaining pasta and filling. (You should have 18 to 20 ravioli.)

Set a large pot of water on the stove to boil.

Walnut and sage butter sauce In a large sauté pan, combine the butter, walnuts and sage over high heat until the butter begins to brown and the milk solids start to foam at the top, about 1 minute. Remove the pan from the heat as soon as this happens, so that the butter won't burn.

Finish ravioli Cook the ravioli in boiling water until they are tender, about 3 minutes. Drain the ravioli and add them to the sauté pan of browned butter and sage. Toss well, then add the cherry tomatoes and arugula. Season with salt and pepper. Spoon onto individual plates and serve garnished with grated Parmesan and a few drops of balsamic vinegar.

 CHEF'S NOTE Feel free to use ricotta cheese instead of goat cheese.

Arugula and goat cheese ravioli

1 c loosely packed arugula

2 Tbsp olive oil

¼ c finely grated Parmesan cheese

¾ c soft goat cheese

1 recipe pasta dough (page 181)

all-purpose flour, for dusting

Walnut and sage butter sauce

⅓ c unsalted butter

½ c coarsely chopped walnuts

12 sage leaves

12 cherry tomatoes, cut in half

⅓ c arugula

grated Parmesan, to garnish

aged balsamic vinegar, to garnish

Perogies were one of the very first foods I learned to cook as a kid. They are a great introduction to making dough because this recipe is so forgiving, and the key to great perogies is the dough. SERVES 6 (16 TO 20 PEROGIES)

Perogies
WITH DILL SOUR CREAM

Perogy dough

2 c all-purpose flour + extra for kneading and rolling dough

½ tsp salt

1 large egg

½ c sour cream + extra to serve with the perogies

¼ c butter, softened and cut into small pieces + more for frying

sprigs of fresh dill for garnish

Caramelized onions

1 tsp butter

1 tsp olive oil

2 onions, sliced

Potato-onion filling

3 Russet potatoes, peeled, boiled and mashed

½ c whipping cream

3 Tbsp butter

2 onions, caramelized (see above)

1 c grated Gruyère cheese

Dill sour cream

⅓ c chopped fresh dill

½ c sour cream

1 Tbsp lemon juice

Perogy dough Place the flour and salt in a large bowl and mix until well combined. In a small bowl, beat the egg, then add it to the flour mixture. Stir in the sour cream and butter. Transfer the mixture to a food processor fitted with a dough hook. Work the dough until it loses most of its stickiness, 5 to 7 minutes. Be careful not to overbeat the mixture. Wrap the dough in plastic wrap and refrigerate for 1 hour or up to 2 days.

Caramelized onions Heat butter and olive oil in a large sauté pan on low heat. Add onions and cook, stirring frequently, until dark brown, about 10 minutes.

Potato-onion filling Place all the ingredients in a large bowl and mix until well combined. Allow to cool completely.

Dill sour cream Place all the ingredients in a small bowl and mix until well combined.

Finish perogies Lightly dust a work surface and a pasta machine with flour. Adjust the pasta machine so the rollers are at the widest setting (usually "0"), then unwrap the dough, flatten it slightly and divide it into 4 sections. Roll one section through the pasta machine. Adjust the pasta machine to the next narrowest setting (usually "1") and pass the dough through the rollers again. Continue to pass the dough through the rollers, adjusting the machine down another setting after each roll until you reach setting 3. (Alternatively, using a rolling pin, roll out the dough to a rectangle 10 inches long by 2½ inches wide by ⅛ inch thick.) Repeat with the remaining dough.

Lightly brush one section of dough with water, then place tablespoonfuls of the potato-onion filling onto the bottom half of the dough, leaving 1 inch between each mound. Fold the top half of the dough over the filling, pinching out any air pockets. Press the edges of the dough together. Using a 2-inch round cookie cutter (or the rim of a glass), cut out the individual perogies. Repeat with the remaining dough and filling.

Bring a large pot of water to a boil over high heat. Add the perogies a few at a time and boil until they float to the top, 2 to 3 minutes. Using a slotted spoon, transfer the cooked perogies to a colander to drain.

While the perogies are boiling, place a cast-iron frying pan over medium-high heat. Stir in a knob of butter and allow it to melt. Add the perogies and fry until golden, about 2 minutes per side. Serve immediately with sour cream and sprigs of fresh dill.

CHEF'S NOTE Perogies freeze <u>very</u> well, so they are a great item to have on hand. To cook from frozen, bring a large pot of salted water to a rapid boil, add perogies and cook for 5 to 7 minutes or until they float to the surface.

ALL ABOUT OLIVE OIL

At the Dirty Apron Cooking School, I get asked a lot about olive oil. It is hugely popular because of all the media reports on the health benefits of olive oil as a monounsaturated fat. It's long been a staple of the Mediterranean diet—right back to Greek and Roman times, in fact—and most olive oil still comes from Spain, Italy and Greece, in that order. American olive orchards are now popping up because of the serious demand south of the border, and there are even olive oil, or "liquid gold," tasting bars for the avid food nerds out there.

Olive oils vary tremendously, so it's imperative that you do some taste testing to know the difference between oils. In my kitchens at Dirty Apron and at home, I've always got two bottles of olive oil on the go. One is for cooking; the other is for dressings and marinades, and for drizzling over salads,

sandwiches, meats and soups. I use a good-quality standard virgin olive oil for cooking. It's great for sautéing mushrooms, garlic or onions, for example. The olive oil for finishing has a bold flavour because it only went through one cold pressing when it was manufactured. This extra-virgin olive oil has a lower acidity and a greener colour, with a big olive taste to match. It's also more expensive than virgin olive oil, which is more processed and acidic, and hasn't got the quality and intensity of flavour.

At the store, I look for olive oils with a low acidity level. If you want to experiment, come by the Dirty Apron for a sample. Because olive oil is such a matter of personal taste, we often crack open bottles for our customers to try.

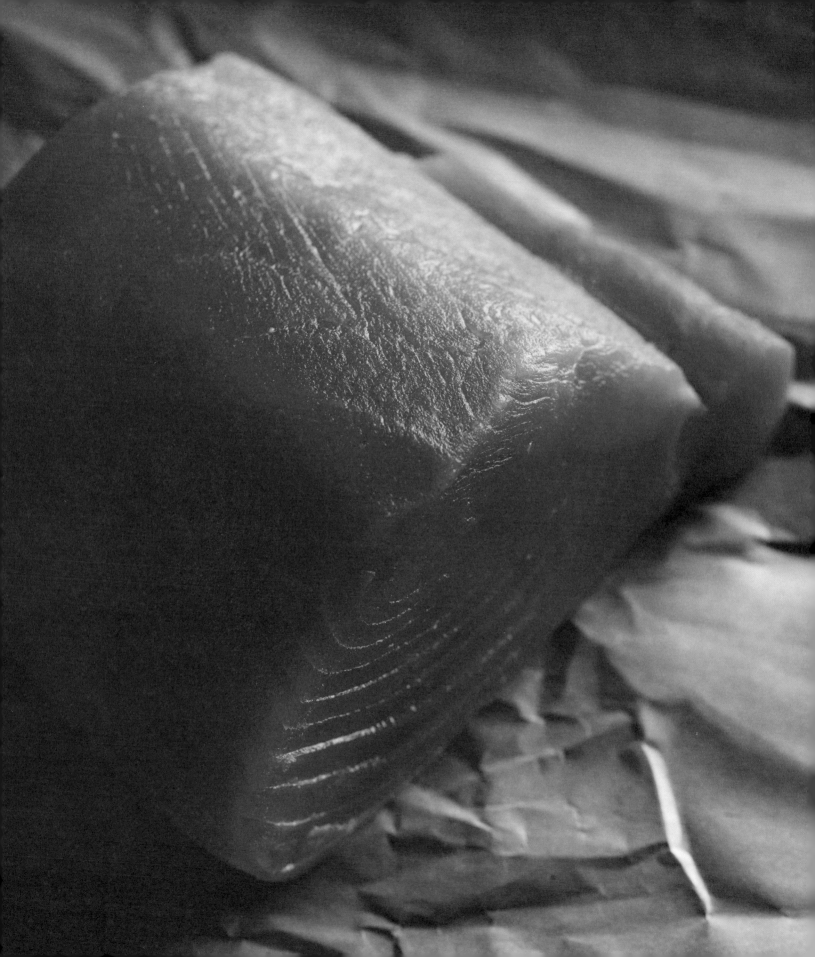

SEAFOOD

GUIDE TO BUYING AND COOKING SEAFOOD

Fish	Texture	Taste	Fresh-Caught	Best Cooking Method	Test for Doneness
Cod	Medium	Mild	April to December	Sautéed, fried, steamed	Done when flakes easily with a fork
Halibut	Firm	Mild	March to November	Baked, sautéed, deep-fried, steamed, poached	Done when flakes easily with a fork
Rainbow trout	Medium	Moderate	Year-round	All cooking methods except steaming	Whole fish should be glistening, moist looking at the innermost core
Ahi tuna	Firm	Moderate	Year-round	Best served rare or seared	Done when the outside of the fish turns light pink and begins to flake slightly
Arctic char	Delicate	Mild	Year-round	Sautéed, broiled, baked, grilled	Done when firm to the touch and greyish in colour
Mahi mahi	Medium to firm	Moderate	Late spring/ early summer	All cooking methods, esp. grilling (holds its moisture well)	Done when flakes easily with a fork
Scallops	Firm	Delicate	Year-round	Best seared on high heat, also grilled, pan-fried, poached, broiled	Turns opaque when done, but centre should be barely opaque
Spot prawns	Firm	Sweet	May through June	Remove heads immediately and rinse tail or meat turns mushy. Cook ASAP. Grilled, sautéed, poached	Done after 1 or 2 minutes, when pink
Clams/mussels	Delicate	Moderate	Year-round	Steamed, baked	Done when fully open
Sockeye salmon	Firm	Full, rich	Year-round	Grilled, baked, steamed, poached, smoked	Darkish pink at centre when cooked medium

I discovered poke on one of our Maui vacations. It's so good that I can easily order a pound at a time and eat only that all day long. Of course, I had to start a Hawaiian cooking class, just so I could show my students how to make it. SERVES 4

Ginger-Soy Tuna Poke on Pressed Avocado

Pressed avocado Halve the avocado and remove and discard the seed. Scoop out ¾ of the avocado flesh and place it in the resealable plastic bag. With the seal of the bag still open, massage the bag with your hands, smashing the avocado and spreading the mashed pulp evenly throughout the bag. You want a mash with an even thickness and no air bubbles. Seal the bag, place it on a baking sheet and set it in the freezer for at least 1 hour.

Ginger-soy tuna poke Place all of the ingredients except the togarashi in a bowl. Mix until well combined. Season to taste with togarashi and salt and pepper.

Finish avocado Remove the avocado from the freezer. Working quickly and using a sharp knife, cut the avocado through the bag into 4 pieces of any shape. Remove and discard the plastic. Set the avocado on individual plates. Top with spoonfuls of the tuna poke and serve immediately. The avocado becomes soft about 2 minutes after it is plated.

CHEF'S NOTES Do your best to keep the tuna cold at all times by keeping it refrigerated before plating. Leaving it at room temperature can cause it to spoil.

Togarashi spice is a seven-spice powder that also includes chilies. It brings out the clean, simple flavours of Japanese food and can be found in specialty Japanese food stores.

Pressed avocado

1 ripe avocado

1 medium resealable plastic bag

Ginger-soy tuna poke

12 oz sushi-grade tuna, in ¼-inch dice

½ c English cucumber, peeled and cut in ⅛-inch dice

1 c finely chopped green onions, white and green parts

juice of 1 lime

2 Tbsp soy sauce

4 tsp sesame seeds, toasted

2 tsp grated fresh ginger

1 tsp sesame oil

togarashi spice, toasted (see Chef's Note)

Do not be intimidated by this flavour combo—it's surprisingly delicious. This recipe was inspired by a dish I fell in love with at Arzak, the famous restaurant in San Sebastián, Spain, that is considered one of the best in the world. Students are always surprised by how delicious this odd-sounding flavour combination turns out to be and how well it works on a salad or served with the Tomato and Lemon Orzo Pasta (page 67). SERVES 4

Cinnamon-Smoked Tuna

1 Tbsp olive oil

½ Tbsp ground cinnamon + a pinch for dusting

4 albacore tuna fillets, each 4 oz

1 cinnamon stick

vegetable oil

Place the olive oil and ground cinnamon in a bowl and whisk well. Set aside.

Place a small wire grill rack in a baking pan. Set the tuna fillets on the rack. Using a lighter or gas burner, carefully light one end of the cinnamon stick and place it on the wire rack beside the tuna. Tightly cover the whole baking pan with aluminum foil. Smoke the tuna in this way for 10 minutes.

Unwrap the baking pan, remove the tuna from the wire rack and season it with salt and pepper and a small pinch or two of ground cinnamon.

Lightly coat a sauté pan with vegetable oil and heat it over high heat. Once the pan is hot, add the tuna and sear it evenly on all sides, 15 to 20 seconds per side. The tuna will have a thin brown sear on the outside but still be rare on the inside.

Transfer the tuna to a plate, brush it with the olive oil and cinnamon mixture and slice each fillet into 3 to 4 pieces. Serve immediately.

 CHEF'S NOTE Make sure you don't smoke the tuna any longer than 10 minutes, or the smoked flavour becomes too strong.

If salmon and trout were to have a baby, it would be Arctic char. This fish dish melts in your mouth: it's got a good balance of lean and fat, and the skin gets beautifully crispy. For anyone afraid of cooking fish, this easy recipe is an excellent place to start. SERVES 4

Arctic Char

WITH VEGETABLE NAGE

Vegetable nage Bring a large pot of lightly salted water to a boil over high heat. Add the vegetables, one variety at a time, and blanch until slightly cooked but still crunchy, 2 to 3 minutes maximum. Using a slotted spoon, transfer the vegetables to a colander to drain. Repeat until all the vegetables have been blanched and drained. Set aside.

Melt ½ Tbsp of the butter in a sauté pan over medium-low heat. Add the garlic and sauté until lightly browned, about 2 minutes. Pour in the stock and allow it to simmer, then reduce the heat to low and whisk in the remaining butter, one cube at a time, until emulsified. Stir in the vegetables and tarragon and season with salt and pepper. Remove from the heat.

Arctic char Pat the fish dry with paper towels and season with salt and pepper. Heat a sauté pan large enough to hold all the fish on high heat. Add enough vegetable oil to lightly coat the bottom of the pan. Once the oil is hot, carefully arrange the fish, skin side down, in the pan and cook without moving it for 2 minutes. The skin should be crispy. Flip the fish over and cook until it flakes when touched with the tip of a knife, about 2 minutes. Stir in the butter and lemon juice, then remove the pan from the heat.

To serve Divide the vegetable nage among the bowls, then top each serving with a fillet of fish. Season to taste with salt and pepper.

Vegetable nage

1 lb vegetables (zucchini, asparagus tips, carrots, etc.), cut into matchsticks

⅓ c unsalted butter, cut into cubes

2 garlic cloves, minced

1 c vegetable stock (page 172)

1 Tbsp fresh tarragon

Arctic char

4 Arctic char fillets, each 5 oz, skin on

vegetable oil

1 Tbsp unsalted butter

juice of ½ lemon

 CHEF'S NOTE Be sure that you allowed the skin to get crispy before flipping the fish over in the pan.

HOW TO BUY FISH

Eric Ripert, chef at Le Bernardin restaurant in New York—arguably one of the best seafood restaurants in the world, says, "The fish is the star of the plate." In other words, he celebrates the fish by enhancing its flavour and texture. Nothing else. So buy the freshest fish you can find.

If you're not catching the fish yourself, then establish a relationship with a good fishmonger who can tell you about the freshest catch of the day. Fresh fish have a shiny, bright skin—nothing dull about it. You want to see bright, clear eyes—nothing milky. And you want bright-red vibrant gills—nothing dull and muted. When you press down on the flesh, your finger shouldn't leave an indentation. That indicates dehydration, as in old fish. Your fish should smell like the sea, no faint whiff of rot. In other words, your fish should look as if it was just plucked from the water. A good fishmonger is your best friend when it comes to advice for cooking fish like an expert.

When buying raw fish for sushi or a ceviche, be sure to source fish that is specially processed for raw consumption. Generally that means the fish has been frozen at –35°C for 15 hours, or at –20°C for 7 days, to kill parasites. The term "sashimi grade," isn't an official guideline, by the way. There is no regulatory body ensuring anything stamped "sashimi grade" or "sushi grade" is guaranteed suitable for raw consumption. That's another reason why you need to make sure you're dealing with a credible fishmonger who knows how to purchase and store seafood.

Check out our seafood chart (page 78) for more information on fish characteristics and cooking times.

Sablefish, also known as butterfish or black cod, is a real West Coast fish. It's easy to cook because it's fatty and moist, which makes salty miso the perfect marinade or glaze. SERVES 4

Miso-Sake Roasted Sablefish

WITH SOY-GINGER VEGETABLES

Miso-sake sablefish In a medium saucepan, bring the sake and mirin to a boil over high heat. Cook for 20 seconds to burn off the alcohol (be careful, as the alcohol may flame). Turn off the heat and whisk in the miso until smooth, then add the sugar. Place the pot back on high heat and bring the mixture to a boil, stirring constantly to be sure the marinade doesn't burn to the bottom of the pot. Remove from the heat and allow to cool.

Arrange the sablefish in a single layer in a casserole dish, cover with the marinade and cover and refrigerate for a minimum of 2 hours or up to 2 days.

Preheat the oven to broil. Line a baking sheet with aluminum foil. Transfer the sablefish to the baking sheet, skin side down, and discard the marinade. Broil the fish on one side for 4 minutes, checking it regularly to be sure it is not burning. (If the sablefish is fully caramelized but not yet cooked, reduce the heat to 375°F and bake for about 3 minutes more.) The total cooking time is 4 to 7 minutes, depending on the thickness of the sablefish fillets. The fish is cooked when it flakes easily with a fork. Remove from the oven and transfer to a plate.

Poached vegetables Combine the dashi, ginger and soy sauce in a medium saucepan over medium heat. Allow the broth to simmer for 3 to 4 minutes to steep the ginger (the longer you steep the ginger, the stronger the flavour). Using a slotted spoon or a tea strainer, remove and discard the ginger.

Add the carrots, soba noodles and edamame and heat over medium heat until warmed through, about 2 minutes. Do not allow this mixture to reduce, or it will become salty.

To serve Arrange the poached vegetables, green onions, mushrooms and noodles in the centre of individual bowls. Carefully pour the broth overtop, then balance the sablefish on the noodles so it is not submerged in the broth. Serve immediately.

Miso-sake sablefish

⅓ c sake

⅓ c mirin (see Chef's Note)

1 c white miso (see Chef's Note)

⅔ c sugar

4 sablefish fillets, each 4 oz, skin on

Poached vegetables

2 c dashi (page 172)

2 Tbsp thinly sliced fresh ginger

2 Tbsp soy sauce

½ c julienned carrots

¼ c soba noodles, cooked

24 shelled edamame beans

½ c julienned green onions

½ c shimeji mushrooms

CHEF'S NOTES The glaze on the sablefish remains very hot after it comes out of the oven. This will allow you a little time to set up the remainder of the dish.

Mirin is a rice wine similar to sake but with less alcohol and more sugar. Miso is a fermented soybean paste. Both are available from Japanese food stores.

The key to this dish is getting a nice brown crust on the halibut by making
sure the pan is hot enough, so high heat is key. SERVES 4

Pan-Roasted Halibut

WITH SAUTÉED SPINACH, CRUSHED FINGERLING
POTATOES AND CHARRED TOMATO VINAIGRETTE

Charred tomato vinaigrette

4 Roma tomatoes

juice of ½ lemon

1 Tbsp sherry vinegar

½ tsp harissa purée

½ tsp cumin seeds,
toasted and ground

¼ c extra-virgin olive oil

Crushed fingerling potatoes

1 lb fingerling potatoes

2 Tbsp olive oil or more

1 Tbsp sliced chives

1 Tbsp finely chopped
Italian parsley

Pan-roasted halibut

4 halibut fillets, each 6 oz

fleur de sel

white pepper

vegetable oil

1 Tbsp unsalted butter

juice of ½ lemon

Sautéed spinach

1 Tbsp unsalted butter

2 garlic cloves, finely chopped

4 c packed spinach, cleaned
and stems trimmed

Charred tomato vinaigrette Preheat a grill to high heat. Set the tomatoes on the grill and cook until the skin is charred and nearly black on all sides, 10 to 15 minutes total. Remove from the grill and allow to cool. Leave the skins on.

Place the tomatoes, lemon juice, vinegar, harissa and cumin in a blender and purée until smooth. Pour the mixture into a bowl, whisk in the olive oil and season with salt and pepper. Will keep refrigerated in an airtight container for up to 1 week.

Crushed fingerling potatoes Preheat the oven to 180°F. Bring a large pot of salted water to a boil on high heat. Add the potatoes and cook until a small knife goes through to the centre. Drain the potatoes, then use a small paring knife to peel the skins while they are still hot. Discard the skins.

Place the potatoes in an ovenproof bowl and crush them with the prongs of a fork. Fold in the olive oil, chives and parsley, mixing gently. Season with salt and pepper. Keep warm in the oven until needed.

Pan-roasted halibut Preheat the oven to 400°F. Season the halibut on both sides with fleur de sel and white pepper.

Heat an ovenproof sauté pan large enough to hold the fish over high heat. Add enough vegetable oil to lightly coat the pan. Place the halibut in the pan, presentation side down. Cook for 1 minute, then place the pan in the oven and cook for 5 to 6 minutes, until the halibut is just cooked through. (The flesh will be opaque and flake slightly.) Remove the pan from the oven. Stir in the butter and lemon juice, then flip the fish over and allow it to rest for 1 minute. The top of the halibut should be a nice golden brown.

Sautéed spinach Melt the butter in a sauté pan over low heat. Add the garlic and cook slowly until slightly browned, about 2 minutes. Stir in the spinach and season with salt and pepper. Cook until tender, about 30 seconds.

To serve Swirl some of the vinaigrette in the middle of each plate. Mound some of the potato on top, then cover with a layer of spinach and a piece of halibut. Serve immediately.

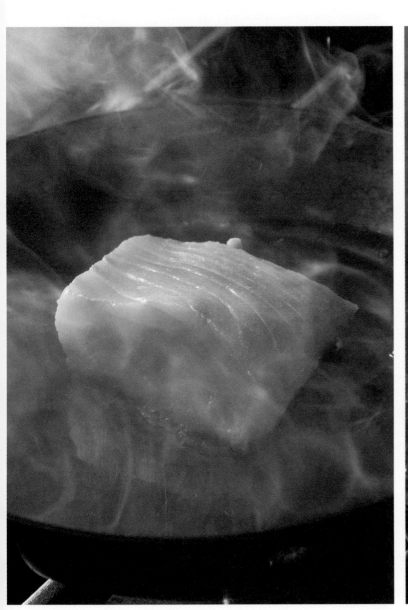

 CHEF'S NOTE You need to maintain your high heat while continuing to sear the halibut on one side. This is where your end result will be a nice golden brown crust.

Halibut cheeks are closer in texture to chicken than to halibut fillets. Because such a meaty piece of fish can handle it, we bring a lot of acidity and a nice fatty aioli to this substantial dish. Serve it with asparagus or crisp green beans. SERVES 4

Pan-Roasted Halibut Cheeks
WITH CITRUS OLIVE OIL–POACHED PRAWNS AND SAFFRON AIOLI

Saffron aioli Put the saffron threads in a small cup, add the hot water and allow to stand for 5 minutes. Place the saffron and water and the remaining ingredients in a small bowl and whisk until smooth. Season to taste with salt and pepper. Will keep refrigerated in an airtight container for up to 1 week.

Citrus olive oil–poached prawns Combine the olive oil, juice and zest from the lemon, lime and orange, and the garlic in a large saucepan. Heat the mixture slowly over medium heat to 135°F. (Use a deep-fat thermometer to measure the temperature.)

Season the prawns with fleur de sel and black pepper, add them to the citrus olive oil and poach until just cooked through, 3 to 4 minutes or until the prawns turn pink. Using a slotted spoon, transfer the prawns to a bowl and cover with plastic wrap. Discard the poaching liquid.

Pan-roasted halibut cheeks Preheat the oven to 180°F. Season the halibut cheeks on both sides with the fennel seeds, coriander seeds, salt and white pepper. Place the flour in a shallow dish. Dredge the halibut cheeks in the flour—shaking off any excess—and set aside on a large plate.

Place a sauté pan on high heat and lightly coat it with the vegetable oil. Add the halibut cheeks and cook until browned on one side, about 2 minutes. Turn the halibut cheeks over and cook for another 2 minutes, until golden. Transfer the halibut cheeks to a large plate and place in the oven to keep warm.

Place a second sauté pan over medium heat, then add the white wine and lemon juice. Bring the mixture to a boil and reduce by half, 2 to 3 minutes. Whisk in the butter, a few cubes at a time, until emulsified. Add the parsley.

To assemble Arrange a spoonful of aioli in the middle of each plate. Cover with halibut cheeks and lean the prawns against them. Spoon some of the lemon butter sauce over the fish. Serve immediately.

CHEF'S NOTES For best results, be careful not to overheat the olive oil.

To avoid overcooking the halibut cheeks, remember that they will cook quite quickly.

Saffron aioli

pinch of saffron threads

1 tsp hot water

½ c mayonnaise

1 garlic clove, minced

½ Tbsp Dijon mustard

juice of ¼ lemon

½ tsp tomato paste

Citrus olive oil–poached prawns

2 c extra-virgin olive oil

juice and zest of 1 lemon

juice and zest of 1 lime

juice and zest of 1 orange

2 garlic cloves, minced

12 16/20 prawns,
shelled and deveined

fleur de sel

black pepper

Pan-roasted halibut cheeks

4 portions halibut
cheeks, each 3 oz

1 Tbsp ground fennel seeds

1 Tbsp ground coriander seeds

½ c all-purpose flour

2 Tbsp vegetable oil

⅓ c white wine

juice of 1 lemon

¼ c unsalted butter,
cut into cubes

2 Tbsp finely chopped
Italian flat-leaf parsley

Anyone worried about overcooking fish, take heart. With this buttery crust on top, the fish soaks up the butter, keeping the fish moist while the crust turns crispy. You can use it on halibut, Arctic char or any other fish. SERVES 4

Citrus and Herb Butter–Crusted Salmon

WITH WHITE BALSAMIC BEURRE BLANC

Herb panko

1 c loosely packed mixed herbs (parsley, basil and chives)

½ c panko crumbs

Citrus and herb butter–crusted salmon

4 skinless, boneless sockeye salmon fillets, each 6 oz

½ c butter, room temperature

1 c herb panko

juice and zest of ½ lemon

White balsamic beurre blanc

1 tsp olive oil

1 shallot, finely diced

¼ c white wine

¼ c white balsamic vinegar

3 Tbsp whipping cream

½ c unsalted butter, cold, in ½-inch cubes

Herb panko Place the herbs in a food processor and mix until finely chopped. Add the panko and blend until the mixture turns green. Set aside. Will keep refrigerated in an airtight container for up to 1 week or frozen for up to 2 months.

Citrus and herb butter–crusted salmon Preheat the oven to 425°F. Line an oven-proof baking pan with parchment paper, then arrange the salmon fillets in a single layer on top.

Combine the butter, herb panko, and lemon juice and zest in a food processor until well mixed. Season to taste with salt and pepper.

Spread the crust mixture over the salmon, then bake for about 8 minutes or until the crust has browned.

White balsamic beurre blanc Heat the olive oil in a small saucepan over medium heat. Add the shallots and sauté until soft, about 2 minutes. Pour in the white wine and vinegar and allow to simmer until only 2 to 3 tablespoons remain. Stir in the cream and simmer for 1 minute.

Using a whisk, vigorously stir in the butter, one cube at a time, until all the butter has been incorporated. Season with salt and pepper. Remove from the heat.

Place a fine chinois over a clean bowl, then strain the sauce through it. Discard the solids.

To serve Arrange the salmon on individual plates and spoon some of the beurre blanc over the fish. Serve immediately.

CHEF'S NOTE The citrus herb butter in this recipe can be frozen and used to crust all types of fish.

Many of my students requested a recipe using mahi mahi, so I responded with this one, which was inspired by our trips to Hawaii. The coconut and chili make a delicious combination with the crushed macadamia nuts and the fennel and papaya salad. SERVES 4

Macadamia Nut–Crusted Mahi Mahi

WITH CHILI COCONUT SAUCE AND FENNEL AND PAPAYA SALAD

Fennel and papaya salad Combine all the ingredients in a medium bowl and toss until well mixed. Season to taste with salt and pepper. Set aside.

Chili coconut sauce Heat the olive oil over medium heat. Add the ginger, garlic and chilies and sauté for 2 minutes. Pour in the fish sauce and stir to deglaze the pan. Immediately add the vegetable stock, coconut milk, palm sugar (or brown sugar) and lemon juice, and bring to a simmer. Continue to simmer until the sauce is thick enough to coat the back of a spoon, 8 to 10 minutes. Stir in the basil and season to taste with salt and pepper.

Macadamia nut–crusted mahi mahi Preheat the oven to 450°F.

Using a food processor, whip the butter and macadamia nuts together until well combined. Add the panko crumbs and blend for 1 minute. Season with salt and pepper.

Season the mahi mahi with salt and pepper and place it on a baking sheet. Using your hands, spread the nut crust over one side of the fish. Bake until the fish flakes when touched with the tip of a knife, 9 to 10 minutes.

To assemble Spoon some of the chili coconut sauce in the middle of each plate. Place the mahi mahi on top and mound several spoonfuls of the papaya and fennel salad alongside. Serve immediately.

 CHEF'S NOTE You can always substitute almonds or other nuts in place of the macadamia nuts.

Fennel and papaya salad

1 large ripe papaya, peeled and seeded

1 fennel bulb, thinly shaved

¼ red onion, thinly sliced

5 sprigs Italian parsley, chopped

3 sprigs Thai basil

juice of ½ lime

3 Tbsp olive oil

Chili coconut sauce

1 Tbsp olive oil

1 tsp minced fresh ginger

2 tsp minced garlic

1 Thai chili, seeds removed, thinly sliced

2 tsp fish sauce

½ c vegetable stock (page 172)

½ c coconut milk

1½ Tbsp palm sugar or brown sugar

juice of ½ lemon

1 Tbsp chopped fresh basil leaves

Macadamia nut–crusted mahi mahi

½ c unsalted butter

½ c macadamia nuts, chopped and toasted until golden

¼ c panko crumbs

4 mahi mahi fillets, each 4 oz

Anyone who's squeamish about eating raw fish will be converted with this dish. The acid of the ceviche and the earthiness of the beets are a delicious pairing. You can switch out the lime for grapefruit juice or use some basil in place of the cilantro if you prefer those flavours. SERVES 4

Grapefruit Lime Scallop Ceviche

WITH GOLDEN BEET CARPACCIO

Scallop ceviche

10 oz 10/20 scallops

1 ear fresh corn, grilled and kernels cut from the cob

12 grape tomatoes, cut into quarters

1 pink grapefruit, peeled and segmented

juice and zest of 2 limes

2 Tbsp very finely sliced cilantro + a few whole leaves for garnish

1 Tbsp finely sliced chives

3 Tbsp extra-virgin olive oil

Golden beet carpaccio

4 medium yellow beets

2 Tbsp extra-virgin olive oil

juice of 1 lemon

Scallop ceviche Slice the scallops very thinly and place them in a large bowl. Add the remaining ingredients and mix gently until well combined. Do not season with salt or pepper. Cover with plastic wrap and refrigerate for up to 30 minutes.

Golden beet carpaccio Place the beets in a large saucepan. Cover them with 2 inches of water and bring to a boil over high heat. Reduce the heat to a gentle simmer and cook until a small knife inserted into the beet comes out with little resistance, about 40 minutes. Drain and allow to stand until cool enough to handle.

Using a very sharp knife, trim off and discard both ends of the beets. Using your fingers, rub off the beet skins and discard. Slice the beets as thinly as possible, using a mandolin or a sharp knife, and place them in a bowl. Add the olive oil and lemon juice and toss to combine. Season with salt and pepper.

Finish ceviche Arrange the beet carpaccio down the middle of each plate. Pour off and discard the ceviche marinade. Season the scallops with salt and pepper. Set them on top of the beet carpaccio. Serve immediately.

 CHEF'S NOTE The key is to not overmarinate the scallops, as the acid of the citrus can "cook" the scallops right through and make them tough.

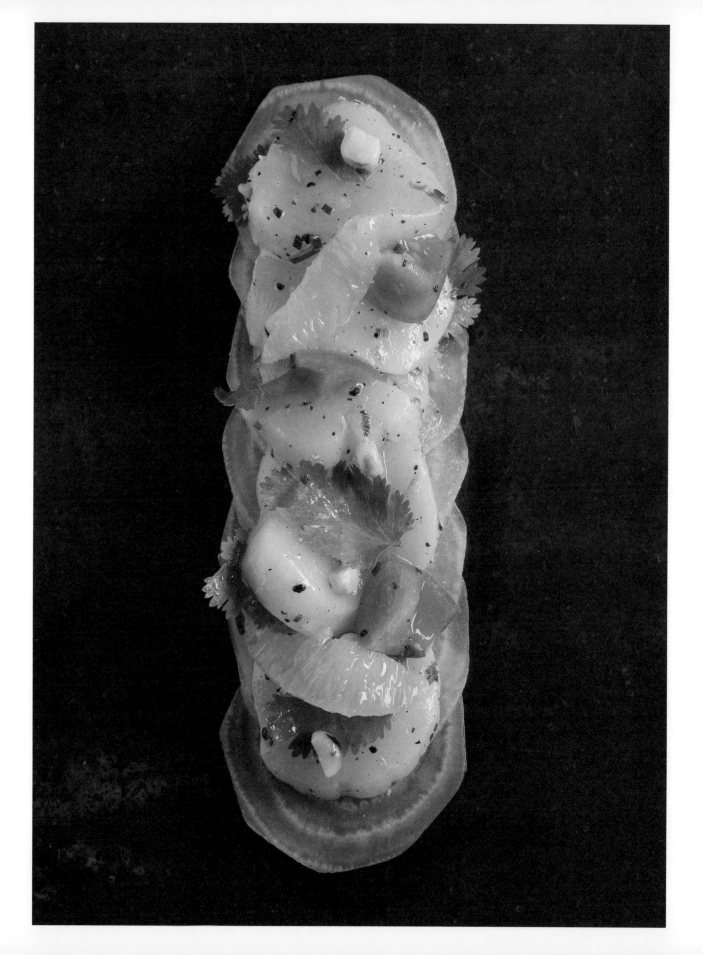

SEAFOOD

I learned this dish during my apprenticeship, and although other chefs have taught me differently, I always come back to this version, made with maple syrup. SERVES 4

Maple-Seared Scallops

WITH WARM CHORIZO AND KALAMATA OLIVE RAGOUT AND PEA COULIS

Pea coulis Heat the olive oil in a small saucepan over medium heat. Add the shallots and garlic and sauté for about a minute. Pour in the vegetable stock and bring to a boil. Stir in the peas and the cream and bring the mixture back to a boil. Remove from the heat and allow to cool slightly.

Using a hand blender, purée the sauce and season it with salt and pepper. (If you prefer a silky smooth coulis, strain it through a fine-mesh sieve.) Will keep refrigerated in an airtight container for 2 to 3 days.

Chorizo and kalamata ragout Heat a small sauté pan over medium heat and add ½ Tbsp of the olive oil to lightly coat the bottom of the pan. Stir in the shallots and chorizo and sauté for 1 minute. Add the olives, chives, lemon juice and 1 Tbsp of olive oil all at once, then remove the pan from the heat. Cover with aluminum foil to keep warm.

Maple-seared scallops Place the scallops in a small bowl and cover them with the maple syrup. Season to taste with salt and pepper.

Heat a small pan over high heat until very hot. Pour in enough vegetable oil to lightly coat the bottom of the pan. Add the scallops and sear on both sides until nicely browned, about 1 minute. The maple syrup will have caramelized.

Reduce the heat to low. Add the butter to the pan and allow it to cook into the scallops, about 1 minute. Using a slotted spoon, transfer the scallops to a plate.

To assemble Spoon the coulis in the middle of each plate. Evenly space 4 scallops in a line over the coulis. Spoon some ragout between the scallops. Serve immediately.

Pea coulis

1 tsp olive oil
1 shallot, finely diced
1 garlic clove, minced
⅔ c vegetable stock (page 172)
1½ c fresh or frozen peas
⅓ c whipping cream

Chorizo and kalamata olive ragout

1½ Tbsp olive oil
1 shallot, diced
½ c diced chorizo sausage
⅓ c kalamata olives, pitted and halved
1 Tbsp sliced chives
juice of ½ lemon

Maple-seared scallops

16 10/20 scallops
¼ c maple syrup
vegetable oil
1 Tbsp unsalted butter

CHEF'S NOTES This coulis works wonderfully hot or cold.

With this dish, don't be afraid to get your pan nice and hot for a good caramelization on the scallop.

SEAFOOD

Dirty Apron chef Takashi developed this recipe for the school, drawing inspiration from the version he ate at home when he was a kid. This pancake is a classic post-war Japanese poor man's dish, from when flour was more abundant than rice. Serve it as an individual meal, share it with a group pizza-style, or cut it up and hand it around as party canapés topped with meats, cheeses, seafood or vegetables. SERVES 4

Okonomiyaki

2 eggs

⅔ c dashi (page 172) or water

1 c all-purpose flour

½ c sliced green onions

2 c julienned white cabbage

grapeseed oil

Suggested toppings and garnishes

6 oz baby shrimp

whole raw spot prawns

scallops, cut in half

asparagus tips

thinly sliced cooked beef, pork or chicken

¼ c okonomiyaki sauce, for garnish

¼ c Japanese mayonnaise, for garnish

¼ c dried seaweed (nori), finely sliced, for garnish

¼ c fine bonito flakes (often sold as *katsuobushi*, or smoked tuna flakes), for garnish

Place the eggs, dashi and flour in a medium bowl and whisk until a smooth batter forms. Season with salt and pepper. In a separate bowl, combine the green onions and cabbage.

Lightly coat a sauté pan with grapeseed oil and heat over medium-high heat. Pour ¼ of the batter into a small bowl. Using a spatula, carefully fold ¼ of the onion-cabbage mixture into the batter, until all the ingredients are mixed in and evenly coated.

Scrape the mixed batter into the pan, allowing it to spread into a circle about ½ inch thick. (The pancake will be about 4 inches wide, but make smaller pancakes if you prefer.) While the pancake is cooking, top with any or all of the suggested toppings. When the bottom edge is beginning to colour, slide a spatula under the pancake and flip it over. Then gently press down on the top of the pancake to even out its thickness. It should still be about ½ inch thick. Cook for about 1 minute more, or until golden and cooked through. Transfer to a plate. Repeat with the remaining batter, green onions, cabbage and toppings until you have 4 pancakes.

Serve the okonomiyaki on individual plates. Drizzle with okonomiyaki sauce and Japanese mayonnaise, and garnish with nori and bonito flakes.

CHEF'S NOTES This is a great way to introduce cabbage to kids. However, you can also substitute other vegetables such as grated zucchini for the cabbage.

It's worth visiting a Japanese specialty store before making this dish, to buy Japanese mayonnaise, nori, bonito flakes and the traditional okonomiyaki sauce, which is basically a combination of Worcestershire sauce and tomato sauce or ketchup.

I created this dish for an Italian cooking class. I wanted to go beyond the straight-ahead ricotta filling and give students something more interesting, to show them how to be a little more creative. The saltiness of the crab balances the sweetness of the ricotta. Serve it with shaved Parmesan cheese as a garnish. SERVES 4

Crab Cannelloni

WITH VINE TOMATO BUTTER SAUCE

Crab cannelloni Preheat the oven to 400°F. Fill a large bowl with cold water.

Bring a large pot of salted water to a boil over high heat. Add the pasta sheets and boil for 1 minute. Using tongs, carefully transfer the cooked sheets to the bowl of cold water and allow to cool. Pat dry with paper towels.

Lightly dust a clean work surface with flour. Arrange the pasta sheets on the counter with the longer side parallel to the edge.

In a bowl, mix together the crab meat, ricotta, pine nuts, lemon zest, chives, thyme, tarragon and Parmesan until well combined. Spoon the mixture into a piping bag fitted with a round tip. Pipe a line of filling along the bottom half of each pasta sheet, right along the edge. Draw the bottom edge of the pasta over the filling, then continue rolling away from you, tightly sealing in the filling, to form a cylinder. Repeat with the remaining cannelloni. Place the filled pasta on a rimmed baking sheet and add the vegetable stock and olive oil. Sprinkle with a bit more Parmesan on top and bake for 10 minutes.

Vine tomato butter sauce Place the tomatoes, vinegar, sugar and basil in a food processor and blend until smooth. Set a fine-mesh sieve over a clean saucepan. Strain the tomato mixture through the sieve, discarding any solids. Cook over medium heat for about 10 minutes, until reduced by half. Using a whisk, beat in the butter until smooth. Season with salt and pepper and set aside.

To serve Spoon some of the tomato sauce onto each plate and cover with the cannelloni.

 CHEF'S NOTE While making the cannelloni, make sure that the pasta is tightly rolled around the crab filling.

Crab cannelloni

1 recipe fresh pasta dough (page 181), cut into 5- × 4-inch rectangles

½ lb crab meat

½ lb ricotta cheese

3 Tbsp pine nuts, toasted

zest of 1 lemon

2 Tbsp finely chopped chives

3 sprigs of thyme

2 Tbsp chopped tarragon

¼ c grated Parmesan cheese + more for the topping

½ c vegetable stock (page 172)

2 Tbsp olive oil

Vine tomato butter sauce

1 lb vine-ripened tomatoes, cut in half

2 tsp sherry vinegar

2 tsp sugar

2 Tbsp chopped fresh basil

⅓ c unsalted butter, cut into cubes

TIPS FOR PLATING AND GARNISHING

Taste trumps trends, gimmicks and show-offy plating. You do want to create a visually appealing dish, but you also want to keep it simple. Be deliberate, not sloppy, when plating food that you took the time to prepare. Show off the components of the dish and arrange them in a way that makes sense. And let your palate be the guide.

When it comes to plating, remember that fish is beautiful on its own. It has great colour and texture, so showcase it, don't complicate it. Instead of mounding your tuna poke until it resembles the Leaning Tower of Pisa, carefully spoon it onto the layer of pressed avocado, showcasing those beautiful colours.

Garnishes, by the way, should always be edible. They are a visual reference to the dish's flavour profile: they hint at what's to come and they add a little punch of taste and colour to the meal. So garnish your plate with flavours that add to the dish—ingredients that are already part of the meal or that complement it—such as a sprinkling of chopped herbs, micro greens, some coarse salt, fried onions or capers, a drizzle of olive oil or honey. These will never distract from or overpower the flavours already on your plate.

POULTRY AND MEATS

TEMPERATURE CHART FOR COOKING MEATS

If you want to be certain of the doneness of your meat and not second-guess yourself, then invest in a good meat thermometer. Always approach the meat from the side as soon as it comes off the heat, inserting the thermometer horizontally into the thickest part of the cut, away from any bones that could throw off the reading. Push the tip of the thermometer as far into the flesh as possible, then slowly draw it out while watching the temperature reading. Some parts of the meat may produce higher readings than others, and that's okay. What you want is a cross-section of readings.

When the lowest reading you get is at the low end of the temperature range for your desired doneness, remove the meat from the heat completely. Set it aside for several minutes to rest, so the meat can relax and the residual heat can finish the cooking. Remember that the larger the cut, the more it will continue to cook while resting.

Type of Meat	Internal Temperature (°F)	Description
POULTRY		
Whole	Breast: 165; Thigh: 165–170	Insert the thermometer in the inner thigh, being careful not to touch the bone, and cook until the juices are clear
Parts	Breast: 165; Thigh: 165–170	
Stuffed	165	
Ground	170–175	
RED MEATS (BEEF, LAMB, DUCK, VENISON), STEAKS AND TENDERLOINS		
Rare	125	Slightly warm, bright red centre but pinkish toward the edges; soft to the touch
Medium-rare	130–135	Warm, very pink in the centre; slightly firm
Medium	140–145	Hot throughout, light pink in the centre; firmer to the touch
Medium-well	150–155	Hot throughout, mostly grey with a hint of pink in the centre; firm to the touch
Ground	160–165	
PORK		
Medium	140–145	Pale pink in the centre
Well Done	160 and higher	Greyish brown throughout
Ground	160	

People always say that these are the best wings they've tasted, hands down. They are also a staff favourite. These are trickier to make than you'd think—the key to getting the meat to slide off the bone is to brine them first. For best results, brine the chicken wings overnight to make them more flavourful and tender. SERVES 6

Southern Fried Chicken Wings

WITH JALAPEÑO CORNBREAD AND HONEY BUTTER

Southern fried chicken wings Remove the chicken wings from the brine, place them in a colander and give them a quick rinse under cold running water. Discard the brine. Pour the buttermilk into a large bowl, submerge the chicken wings and allow them to soak for 2 hours.

Honey butter Place the butter and honey in a small bowl and combine until evenly mixed. Set aside.

Jalapeño cornbread Preheat the oven to 425°F. Lightly grease a 12-hole muffin tin.

Combine the flour, cornmeal, sugar, salt, baking powder and baking soda in a large bowl. In a separate bowl, beat together the buttermilk, butter, egg and jalapeño pepper until well mixed. Slowly stir the dry ingredients into the buttermilk mixture, whisking gently to break up any lumps. Pour the batter into the muffin tin, filling each one about ⅔ full. (You should have 12 large muffins.) Bake for 18 minutes, or until a knife inserted in the centre comes out clean.

Finish chicken wings Heat the canola oil in a large pot on medium heat until it reaches 375°F. (Use a deep-fat thermometer to check the temperature.) Line a plate with paper towels.

In a large bowl, combine the flour and all of the spices until well mixed. One by one, remove the wings from the buttermilk, dredge them in the flour mixture (making sure you get a nice thick and even coating on the wing) and drop them gently into the oil. Cook until the chicken has fried to a deep golden brown, about 7 minutes. Using tongs, transfer the cooked chicken to the paper towel–lined plate to drain.

To serve Serve family style in a bucket, or arrange 5 wings per person on individual plates, with warm jalapeño cornbread and honey butter.

 CHEF'S NOTE For this recipe, brining the wings makes a big difference because it locks in all the moisture, giving you a very juicy final product.

Southern fried chicken wings

30 chicken wings, brined overnight in spiced brine (page 174)
4 c buttermilk
4 c canola oil
3 c all-purpose flour
2 Tbsp chili powder
2 Tbsp mustard powder
1 Tbsp garlic powder
1 Tbsp onion powder
1 Tbsp smoked paprika
1 Tbsp salt
1 Tbsp pepper

Honey butter

½ c butter, room temperature
⅓ c honey

Jalapeño cornbread

1 c all-purpose flour
½ c cornmeal
2 Tbsp sugar
1 tsp salt
1 tsp baking powder
1 tsp baking soda
¾ c buttermilk
½ c melted butter
1 egg
1 jalapeño pepper, finely chopped

This Mediterranean dish was created by one of my chefs, Olivia, and reminds me of my childhood because my parents made a lot of braises and stews. For texture, it's hard to beat the fall-off-the-bone quality of this meat. SERVES 6

Chicken Marbella

WITH RICE PILAF

Chicken Marbella

6 chicken legs, skin on, brined overnight in classic brine (page 174)

vegetable oil

1 Tbsp olive oil

1 medium onion, diced

6 bay leaves

5 garlic cloves, minced

¼ c fresh thyme (whole sprigs)

¼ c fresh oregano (whole sprigs)

1 cinnamon stick

1 tsp cayenne pepper

2½ c white wine

2½ c chicken stock (page 173)

¼ c capers

20 prunes, pitted

¼ c kalamata olives, pitted

4 Tbsp brown sugar

juice and zest of 1 lemon

1 c fresh Italian parsley

Rice pilaf

1 Tbsp canola oil

1 onion, peeled and
cut in small dice

1 carrot, peeled and
cut in small dice

2 celery stalks, in small dice

2 garlic cloves, minced

3 bay leaves

2 c long-grain white basmati rice

2½ c chicken stock (page 173)

1 Tbsp unsalted butter

Chicken Marbella Preheat the oven to 400°F. Remove the chicken legs from the brine, pat them dry with paper towels and season generously with salt and pepper. Discard the brine.

Heat a large sauté pan over high heat. Add enough vegetable oil to coat the bottom of the pan. Add the chicken legs, skin side down, and sear on all sides until golden, about 8 minutes total. (Do not overcrowd the pan; cook the chicken in batches, if necessary.) Transfer the chicken legs to an ovenproof pan large and deep enough to hold them all and set aside.

Heat the olive oil in a sauté pan over medium heat. Add the onions and bay leaves, season with salt and pepper and cook for 1 minute. Stir in the garlic, thyme, oregano, cinnamon stick and cayenne and cook, stirring continuously, for another 8 minutes. Pour in the white wine and bring to a boil. Add the chicken stock, bring back to the boil and then remove from the heat. Pour the broth over the chicken until it reaches ¾ of the way up the meat (add extra stock, if necessary). Sprinkle the capers, prunes, olives and brown sugar all over the chicken, then bake, uncovered, for 1 hour.

Rice pilaf Heat the canola oil in a large pot over medium heat. Add the onions, carrots, celery, garlic and bay leaves, season with salt and pepper and sauté for 3 to 4 minutes. Stir in the rice, then pour in the chicken stock and reduce the heat to medium-low. Cover and cook for 20 to 30 minutes, or until all the liquid has evaporated. Remove from the heat, stir in the butter, then cover again and set aside.

To serve Mound the rice pilaf on individual plates. Set the chicken on the rice, then spoon the pan juices over each serving. Garnish with the lemon juice, lemon zest and parsley.

 CHEF'S NOTE While your chicken is cooking, start on your rice pilaf. Or prepare this dish up to 2 days in advance; it tastes better with each passing day.

Brining is the secret to incredibly moist, succulent poultry. At the Dirty Apron, we brine a lot of our poultry, and it's worth the small amount of effort that it requires. It is easy, economical and infuses the food with a level of flavour you can't get by merely cooking. I swear by it. And given its popularity right now—everything from fish to cheese to vegetables is being given the brining treatment—others do too.

A brining solution is similar to a marinade, but it's the salt content that makes the difference. The salt alters the structure of the protein so that it draws in and holds on to the water. A lot of that water will be drawn back out during cooking, but a lot of it will be retained too—making for an ultra juicy, tender piece of meat. A brine, then, starts with salt and water. Generally speaking, the ratio is about two tablespoons of salt to four cups of water. You can also get creative with the flavourings you add to it: try cider or rice wine vinegar, citrus juices, beer, soy sauce, tea, sugar, molasses, honey, bay leaves, orange slices, crushed garlic, cloves, cinnamon stick, any number of spices. To figure out ratios, follow our brine recipes here in the book (pages 126 and 174) and switch out any spices or ingredients to create your own flavours.

Refrigeration is key throughout the entire brining process. Ensure that all brining liquid is cold, or 39°F, before you put the meat into it. For example, if you need to cook down the sugar for a brine, be sure to chill it to 39°F before using it. Unless you have an industrial refrigerator that can hold a five-gallon bucket to brine a turkey, the easiest method is to use plastic brining bags. They come in sizes that can hold a turkey. Once filled and sealed and refrigerated, just be sure to give the bag a turn now and then to ensure a thorough brine.

Brine times vary, but if you are new to the method, you probably want to be cautious and go for less time. Brining does make the meat saltier, and once it's brined, you can't undo the salt content. Also, the bigger the piece of poultry, the longer you need to brine it. In other words, a chicken breast needs less brining time than a whole turkey. Generally, it's a good rule to brine for a minimum of one hour per pound of poultry. For example, a four-pound chicken can take anywhere from four to twelve hours of brine time.

The bottom line is that any brining is better than none. Believe me, when it comes to cooking meat, brining will change your world.

Turkey dinner can be an elaborate undertaking for a lot of people, so I teach my students how to simplify turkey dinners. Brining is one way to ensure a moist bird, and it's easy—it just takes preparation. And the stuffed turkey legs are a bonus that will blow everyone away. SERVES 12

Roasted Turkey Breast and Boneless Roasted Stuffed Turkey Leg

WITH CRANBERRY COMPOTE

Cranberry compote Place the cranberries, orange juice and zest, lemon juice and zest, sugar, red wine and water in a medium saucepan and bring to a boil over medium-high heat. Cook for about 5 minutes. Pour in the cornstarch mixture, reduce the heat to low and stir constantly until the mixture thickens. Add the thyme and set aside.

Roasted and stuffed turkey Preheat the oven to 400°F.

Begin by removing the turkey legs. To do this, hold the thigh and slide a boning knife along the inside of the thigh against the breast. Continue to slide the knife down all the way to the joint, then pull the thigh away from the breast with your hands. When the round end of the thighbone is visible, cut through the joint to detach the thigh. Repeat on the other side. Wrap the legs tightly in plastic wrap and refrigerate until needed. Remove and set aside the giblets, then rinse the turkey and pat it dry with paper towels.

Season the turkey inside and out with 1 Tbsp of the smoked paprika and some salt and pepper. Rub 2 Tbsp of the butter, lemon juice and vegetable oil over the turkey breast.

Place the turkey breast and giblets in a roasting pan and cook for 1½ to 2 hours or until the turkey is golden and the juices run clear. (To test for doneness, insert an instant-read thermometer into the thickest part of the meat; it should read 165°F.) Remove from the oven, transfer the turkey to a plate and allow to rest for 30 minutes. Reserve the giblets and the pan juices for gravy.   *continued overleaf >*

Cranberry compote

½ lb cranberries (fresh or frozen)

juice and zest of 1 orange

juice and zest of 1 lemon

½ c sugar

¼ c dry red wine

1½ c water

2 Tbsp cornstarch mixed with 4 Tbsp cold water

1 Tbsp chopped fresh thyme

Roasted and stuffed turkey

1 turkey, 12 to 15 lbs

2 Tbsp smoked paprika

5 Tbsp unsalted butter

juice of 1 lemon

2 Tbsp vegetable oil

CHEF'S NOTES Prepare the compote a day ahead to allow the cranberries to soak up all the flavour of the added ingredients. It will also go very well with your next cheese platter or dessert.

For added flavour and a juicier turkey, you can brine it for 24 hours in classic brine (page 174) before starting this recipe. Allowing the turkey to rest for a solid 30 minutes before even thinking about carving it results in a much juicier turkey.

Gravy

4 Tbsp all-purpose flour

4 c chicken stock (page 173)

2 sprigs of Italian parsley, leaves only

2 sprigs of thyme, leaves only

Chestnut and apple stuffing

¼ c unsalted butter

1 white onion, finely diced

2 garlic cloves, chopped

2 celery stalks, in ¼-inch dice

3 c chestnuts (about 1 lb), peeled, roasted and cut in half

2 Granny Smith apples, peeled and cut in ½-inch dice

6 c day-old brioche bread (page 17) or Pullman loaf, crusts removed, cut into ½-inch cubes

¼ c chicken stock (page 173)

¼ c whipping cream

4 sprigs of thyme, chopped

4 sprigs of sage, chopped

4 sprigs of Italian parsley, chopped

Gravy Remove the giblets from the pan and set aside. Pour the pan juices into a medium saucepan, bring to a boil over medium heat and cook until they have caramelized, 2 to 3 minutes. Pour off all but 4 tablespoons of the fat. Reduce the heat to medium-low.

Sprinkle the flour into the pan and stir for 1 minute. Using a whisk, add the chicken stock a little at a time until the gravy thickens and becomes smooth. Season with salt and pepper, then strain into a clean saucepan. Reserve the giblets to make soup.

Chestnut and apple stuffing Preheat the oven to 400°F.

Melt the butter in a large saucepan over medium heat, then add the onions, garlic, celery and chestnuts and sauté for about 3 minutes. Stir in the apples and bread, cook for another 2 minutes, then add the chicken stock, cream and all the herbs. Season with salt and pepper. Spread the stuffing into a shallow baking dish and bake, uncovered, until the top is golden, about 20 minutes. Remove from the oven and allow to cool before stuffing the turkey legs.

Finish turkey Preheat the oven to 400°F. Cut 2 squares of aluminum foil large enough to hold the turkey legs. Unwrap the turkey legs. Using a boning knife, hold a turkey leg and run the knife along the side of the bone to separate the meat from the bone. Try to keep the meat in one long piece. Repeat with the second turkey leg. (Reserve the bones to make stock.)

Place the meat on a clean work surface and season with 1 Tbsp of smoked paprika and salt and pepper. Arrange ¼ of the stuffing down the centre of each piece of leg meat. (Spoon the leftover stuffing into a small casserole dish.) Tightly roll the leg meat over the stuffing. Rub ½ of the remaining butter on each piece of foil, then rub the foil over the turkey rolls. Place a rolled turkey leg onto each piece of foil. Fold the bottom half of the foil over the turkey leg, then the top half and fold in the ends as if you were wrapping a parcel, ensuring the turkey legs are tightly wrapped. Set the foil-wrapped legs in a roasting pan and cook for 25 minutes. (Cook the stuffing in the casserole dish at the same time.) Remove the turkey from the oven, unwrap and discard the foil and cook the meat unwrapped until the legs are fully cooked. (To test for doneness, insert an instant-read thermometer into the thickest part of the meat; it should read 165°F.) Reserve any pan juices to add to the gravy.

To serve Arrange the turkey on a large platter. Reheat the gravy, stirring in the parsley and thyme just before serving, then pour into a gravy boat. Spoon the compote into a serving bowl. Serve the gravy, compote and stuffing alongside the turkey.

CHEF'S NOTES There are other stuffing options: add bacon or try other herbs such as oregano, marjoram or rosemary. Have fun with this recipe.

If you are not confident deboning the turkey leg yourself, ask your butcher to do it for you.

Duck is one of my all-time favourite foods. It's a really versatile meat. I like to say that if you can master the art of cooking duck meat, everything else will be easy. SERVES 4

Crispy Seared Duck Breast

WITH ORANGE GASTRIQUE AND APPLE AND GREEN BEAN SAUTÉ

Crispy seared duck breast Using a sharp knife, trim the duck breast of excess fat and sinew and discard. Score the remaining fat (not the meat) at ¼-inch intervals, first in one direction, then at 90° to the original cuts to create a cross-hatch pattern.

Place the orange zest, cinnamon, cardamom, maple syrup, pepper and olive oil in a bowl large enough to hold the duck, and mix until well combined. Add the duck and allow to marinate for at least 2 hours or up to 12 hours.

Remove the duck from the marinade, wipe off the spices with a paper towel and pat dry. Season with salt and pepper. Discard the marinade. Heat a large pan over medium heat, add the duck, skin side down, and cook for 7 to 8 minutes. If the skin is browning too quickly, reduce the heat; if it is not browning, increase the heat. The skin should be brown and crisp. Turn the duck over and brown the flesh side for about 2 minutes. Remove from the heat and allow the duck to rest in the pan for 5 minutes.

Orange gastrique Place the honey and vinegar in a saucepan over medium heat and simmer until reduced by half, 3 to 4 minutes. Pour in the Grand Marnier, orange juice and lemon juice and reduce by half again, 2 to 3 minutes. Remove the pan from the heat and whisk in the butter, one cube at a time, until well emulsified. Set aside.

Apple and green bean sauté Fill a large bowl with ice and cold water. Bring a pot of salted water to a boil over high heat, add the beans and cook for 2 minutes or until just crisp-tender. Plunge them into the ice bath to stop the cooking and keep them green.

Melt the butter in a small sauté pan over low heat, add the apples and sauté for about 1 minute. Stir in the green beans, sauté for another minute and season with salt and pepper.

To serve Set the duck breasts, skin side down, on a cutting board. Holding a sharp knife at an angle, slice the duck diagonally into 8 slices. Spoon some of the apple and green bean sauté onto individual plates. Fan a couple of slices of the duck, skin side up, over the sauté, drizzle with the orange gastrique and sprinkle with Maldon salt.

Crispy seared duck breast

4 duck breasts, each 8 oz

zest of 1 orange

1 tsp cinnamon

1 tsp green cardamom pods, crushed

2 Tbsp maple syrup

1 tsp black pepper

⅓ c olive oil

Maldon salt

Orange gastrique

½ c honey

½ c sherry vinegar

2 Tbsp Grand Marnier

2 Tbsp orange juice

2 Tbsp lemon juice

⅓ c unsalted butter, cut into cubes

Apple and green bean sauté

3 oz French green beans, stalk ends trimmed

½ Tbsp butter

½ Granny Smith apple, cored and diced

 CHEF'S NOTE As the duck is cooking, be sure to check it as often as possible to ensure that the fat is rendering down properly.

This dish was inspired by my travels through Tuscany. When a recipe resonates with me, I bring it back to the Dirty Apron and see if I can use it in a class. SERVES 4

Porcini-Rubbed Pork Tenderloin

WITH SAUTÉED FINGERLING POTATOES
AND CIPOLLINI ONIONS AND SALSA VERDE

Porcini-rubbed pork

¼ c dried porcini mushrooms, ground to a fine powder

¼ c brown sugar

1 Tbsp olive oil

1 Tbsp red pepper flakes

4 pieces of pork tenderloin, each 6 oz

Sautéed fingerling potatoes and cipollini onions

½ lb fingerling potatoes

3 oz green beans, stalk ends trimmed

1 Tbsp vegetable oil

12 cipollini onions

4 oz double-smoked bacon, in ¼-inch cubes

¼ c Cinzano (sweet red vermouth)

1 Tbsp red wine vinegar

3 Tbsp extra-virgin olive oil

4 sprigs of Italian parsley (optional)

Salsa verde

1 small garlic clove, peeled

1 Tbsp baby capers, rinsed and roughly chopped

2 anchovy fillets, very finely chopped

½ c Italian parsley leaves, washed and roughly chopped

1 Tbsp mint leaves, washed and roughly chopped

1 Tbsp Dijon mustard

⅓ c extra-virgin olive oil

red wine vinegar, to taste

Porcini-rubbed pork In a small bowl, stir together the porcini powder, brown sugar, olive oil and red pepper flakes until well combined. Rub the mixture over the pork tenderloins, using as much as possible to coat the meat evenly. Place the pork in a large bowl and refrigerate, covered, for 12 to 24 hours.

Preheat a grill to high heat. Remove the pork from the bowl, brushing off the excess marinade, and season with salt and pepper. Place the pork on the grill and cook, turning every few minutes, for 8 to 10 minutes for medium-rare, or longer if you prefer your meat medium or well done. Remove from the heat and set aside.

Fingerling potatoes and cipollini onions Bring a large pot of salted water to a boil over high heat. Add the potatoes and cook for 3 minutes, or until a small knife goes through to the centre. Drain the potatoes and cut into thick round slices. Set aside.

Fill a bowl with ice and cold water. Bring a pot of water to a boil over high heat, add the green beans and cook for about 2 minutes, until tender but not cooked through. Transfer the beans to the ice bath to stop the cooking, then drain and set aside.

Heat the vegetable oil in a sauté pan over medium heat. Add the onions and bacon and cook slowly until both are golden, 4 to 5 minutes. Stir in the potatoes, green beans, Cinzano and vinegar and cook until the liquid coats the vegetables, about 1 minute. Finish with extra-virgin olive oil. Season with salt and pepper.

Salsa verde Chop the garlic with a little pinch of salt until you reach a paste-like consistency. Place the garlic, capers and anchovies in a small bowl. Add the parsley, mint and Dijon mustard and stir well to combine. Slowly add the olive oil in a continuous stream, using a whisk to combine the salsa. Season with the vinegar and salt and pepper to taste. Will keep refrigerated in an airtight container for up to 3 days.

To serve Divide the potatoes and green beans among individual plates. Place slices of pork on top and finish with the salsa verde. Garnish with a sprig of parsley.

CHEF'S NOTES Keep a close eye on the pork while it is on the grill, as the sugar in the marinade can char if the grill is too hot.

This is my go-to sauce because it can be served with absolutely everything: fish, meat, poultry, pasta, salads, etc.

This recipe is a finger licker that we teach to illustrate the value of cooking meat on the bone. At the Dirty Apron we are big believers in brining, and it's worth the effort for this dish because the ribs are addictive. Start the brining the day before you plan to serve these ribs. SERVES 4

Hoisin-Glazed Ribs

WITH ASIAN SESAME SLAW

Brined ribs

2 whole racks of baby pork ribs, about 3 lbs

4 c water

1 whole star anise

1 garlic clove, crushed

2 strips of lemon zest

5 black peppercorns

1 bay leaf

1 cinnamon stick

2 Tbsp salt

1 Tbsp coriander seeds

½ jalapeño pepper, coarsely chopped

5 to 6 sprigs fresh cilantro

2 green onions, julienned

1 Tbsp sesame seeds

Hoisin glaze

1 c hoisin sauce

1 tsp sesame oil

1 tsp sambal oelek

1 Tbsp soy sauce

Asian sesame slaw

3 c very thinly sliced green cabbage

1½ c shredded carrots

1 c fresh spinach, trimmed

¼ c rice vinegar

2 Tbsp sesame oil

2 Tbsp sugar

1 Tbsp minced fresh ginger

1½ Tbsp soy sauce

Brined ribs Cut each of the whole racks of ribs in half, so you have 4 pieces. Pat dry the ribs with a paper towel. Using a dry cloth, grasp the underside of the rib and pull very carefully to remove the membrane from the back of the ribs. Discard the membrane. Set aside.

To prepare the brine, bring the water to a boil in a large pot over high heat, turn off the heat and add the star anise, garlic, lemon zest, peppercorns, bay leaf, cinnamon stick, salt, coriander seeds and jalapeño peppers. Allow to cool slightly, then refrigerate until the brine reaches 39°F, about 1 hour. Place the ribs into the brine and refrigerate for 24 hours.

Remove the rib racks from the brine and cut them into individual ribs. Discard the brine. Place the ribs into a large pot, cover completely with cold water and bring to a boil over high heat. Reduce the heat to medium-low and simmer for 1 to 1¼ hours, or until the ribs are soft but not yet falling off the bone. Allow the ribs to cool in their cooking liquid.

Hoisin glaze Place all the ingredients in a bowl and mix together until well combined. Will keep refrigerated in an airtight container for up to 2 weeks.

Asian sesame slaw Combine the cabbage, carrots and spinach in a large bowl.

In a medium bowl, whisk together the vinegar, sesame oil, sugar, ginger and soy sauce until the sugar dissolves. Season to taste with salt and pepper. Pour the dressing over the vegetables, toss until well coated, then season with salt and pepper.

Finish ribs Preheat a barbecue to high or set your oven to broil. (If you use the oven, place the glazed ribs on a baking sheet.) Remove the cooled ribs from their cooking liquid, brush them liberally with glaze, and grill or broil until the glaze has cooked on, about 1 minute.

To serve Serve the ribs on individual plates and garnish with cilantro, green onions and sesame seeds, and generous servings of Asian sesame slaw.

 CHEF'S NOTE The vegetables can be assembled and the dressing assembled the day before you plan to serve the salad. Cover them separately and mix them just before serving.

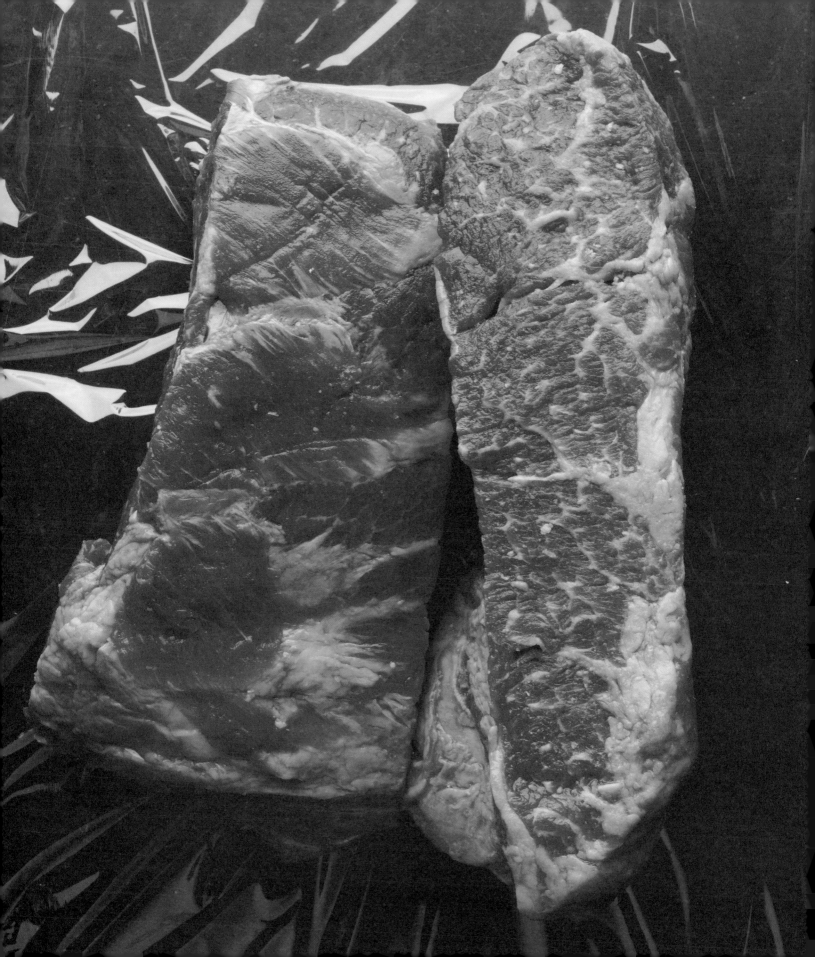

Nothing gets me more excited than a good steak. And as a chef, I've learned that the most expensive cuts of meat, such as the tenderloin, aren't necessarily the tastiest. That's why it's in every cook's interest to learn how to work with secondary cuts of meat, those inexpensive cuts that our moms relied on to keep a hungry family going on a shoestring budget.

Today, nose-to-tail cooking has put the focus on secondary cuts such as flank steak, short ribs, pork belly and shanks. They may take longer to cook, but the result can be more delicious, tender and succulent than quicker-cooking primary cuts. And they're a great way to learn how to cook meat. If you go to your local butcher shop and try out a different inexpensive cut each week—be it lamb, pork, beef or game meat, like venison— you'll become a skilled cook of meats in no time. Get to know the body parts so you know how to cook them. A tougher meat such as a beef short rib needs to be slowly braised to break down the connective tissue, whereas tenderloin or rib-eye cuts don't need such preparation.

As a chef, I find secondary cuts far more exciting to work with because I can show off my technique. Any chef can work with tenderloin. But having the skill and patience to turn a shank or short rib into its fall-off-the-bone equivalent is doing something truly special. It means messing around with different cooking temperatures and methods, such as braising, roasting, searing and grilling. If it's a secondary cut of beef, the challenge is to make it tender and juicy. If it's a fatty piece of pork belly, it means rendering it down so that the fat comes out super crispy. Preparing the meat, be it brining or marinating it, makes a difference to any secondary cut.

And don't ignore the juices that accumulate at the bottom of the pan. Drizzle some of the pan juices or some of the sauce from the Chicken Marbella (page 114) or Braised Beef Short Ribs (page 130) across the rice or risotto before serving. Remember that the biggest flavours are often at the bottom or sides of the pan—those crispy bits of a grilled chop, or the bits of meat that have joined the sauce after a long braising. Don't be stingy. Add them to the plate. That's the best flavour. That's what you want.

As a chef, it's easy to use tenderloin because it's already tender. But it's more fun and more of a challenge to take a short rib, braise it and infuse it with big flavours, which is what we do here. Serve with the risotto, potatoes or even a salad. SERVES 6

Braised Beef Short Ribs

WITH MOREL AND THYME RISOTTO

Braised short ribs

vegetable oil

6 beef short ribs, each 8 to 10 oz

2 large onions, diced

1 head of garlic, peeled and chopped

3 c dry red wine

6 c beef stock (page 173)

½ c maple syrup

¼ c sherry vinegar

2 bay leaves

1 bunch of fresh thyme

Morel and thyme risotto

4 c vegetable stock (page 172)

2 Tbsp olive oil

2 shallots, finely diced

2 cloves garlic, minced

1¼ c carnaroli or arborio rice

¼ c dry white wine

1 oz dried morels, soaked in water and drained

¼ c butter

8 sprigs Italian parsley, leaves only, finely chopped

4 sprigs thyme, leaves only, finely chopped

truffle oil, to taste

⅓ c grated Parmesan cheese

1 chunk Parmesan cheese for grating, for garnish

Braised short ribs Preheat the oven to 350°F. Heat a large sauté pan over high heat and add enough vegetable oil to coat the pan. Season the short ribs on all sides with salt and pepper. When the oil is very hot and almost smoking, carefully add the short ribs and sear until browned on all sides, about 2 minutes. Transfer the ribs to a braising pan. Reduce the heat to medium.

Add the onions and garlic to the sauté pan and cook until tender, about 5 minutes. Add the red wine and cook, scraping any leftover bits of meat from the bottom of the pan, until reduced by half, 8 to 10 minutes. Stir in the beef stock, maple syrup and vinegar and bring to a boil, then pour the boiling liquid over the short ribs. The liquid should almost cover the ribs (add stock or water, if it does not). Add the bay leaves and thyme. Cover the braising pan tightly with aluminum foil and braise for about 4 hours, or until the meat is fork-tender.

Morel and thyme risotto Heat the stock in a medium pot over medium-high heat.

In another medium pot, heat the olive oil over low heat. Add the shallots and garlic and cook very slowly for about 2 minutes. Add the rice, stirring continuously, and increase the heat to medium. Continue stirring the rice for about 1 minute. Pour in the white wine, stirring continuously, until it has been absorbed, about 2 minutes.

Add a ladleful of the hot stock and a pinch of salt. Reduce the heat to a simmer and allow to cook, still stirring, until all the liquid has been absorbed. Continue adding stock, one ladleful at a time, and allowing it to be completely absorbed. Repeat for about 15 minutes. Check the rice to see if it is cooked. If not, keep adding stock (or boiling water) until the rice is soft but has a slight bite.

Stir in the morels and continue cooking for another minute. Season to taste with salt and pepper, then remove from the heat and add the butter, parsley, thyme, truffle oil and grated Parmesan. Stir well. Remove from the oven.

Finish short ribs Remove the pan from the oven and place over medium-high heat to allow the sauce to thicken slightly. Season to taste with salt and pepper.

To serve Divide the risotto among individual plates, place short ribs on top and spoon some of the sauce over the meat. Garnish with Parmesan cheese and serve immediately.

 CHEF'S NOTE Always make sure that your braising liquid is at a gentle simmer, not boiling. Top it up with a little stock or water if it starts to dry out.

This French classic reminds me of my father bringing home different meats from the butcher shop and my mom braising them in the old-school Crock-Pot. Garnish this dish with chopped parsley and serve it alongside boiled potatoes, rice or buttered noodles. SERVES 4

Boeuf Bourguignon

1 Tbsp vegetable oil

1 lb chunk of bacon, in 1-inch dice

2 lbs lean stewing beef, in 2-inch dice

⅔ onion, sliced

1 c sliced carrots

4 garlic cloves, minced

16 small white pearl onions

1½ Tbsp all-purpose flour

2 c red wine

4 c beef stock (page 173)

2 tsp tomato paste

4 sprigs of thyme

1 bay leaf

¼ lb mushrooms, sautéed, for garnish

Preheat the oven to 375°F. Line a large plate with paper towels.

Heat the vegetable oil in a medium ovenproof saucepan over medium heat. Add the bacon and sauté until lightly browned, 4 to 5 minutes. Using a slotted spoon, transfer the bacon to the paper towel–lined plate to drain. Set aside the pan with the bacon fat.

Pat dry the beef with a paper towel and season with salt and pepper. Place the pan with the bacon fat over high heat until the fat is almost smoking. Add the beef and cook until nicely browned on all sides, about 2 minutes. Transfer the beef to the plate with the bacon.

To the same pan, add the sliced onions, carrots, garlic and pearl onions and cook over low heat until browned, about 2 minutes. Carefully pour off the fat, leaving the vegetables in the pan, and add the beef and bacon. Sprinkle the flour over the meat then stir in the red wine and stock until the meat is just covered. Add the tomato paste and herbs. Bring the mixture to a simmer, then cover and cook in the oven for 2 to 2½ hours, or until the meat is fork-tender. Remove the pan from the oven and add the mushrooms.

Using a spoon, skim the fat from the surface, then set over medium heat and simmer for another minute, skimming off any additional fat that rises. Remove the bay leaf and thyme. Season to taste with salt and pepper.

 CHEF'S NOTE This is another great dish that can be prepared a day ahead.

It took me a while to learn how to properly prepare venison, which is a very lean meat and can easily dry out, but it's well worth the effort. The trick to great venison is adding some fat to the dish. SERVES 4

Venison Chop

WITH CELERIAC PURÉE

Venison chop Arrange the bacon slices on a clean work surface. Place a prune at one end of each slice, and wrap the bacon tightly around it. Set aside. Season the venison with salt and pepper.

Heat a medium pan over medium-high heat. Add the vegetable oil, then sear the venison on one side, about 1 minute. Turn over the venison, reduce the heat to medium-low and add the butter and bacon-wrapped prunes. Cook until the venison is done, 4 to 5 minutes for medium-rare, or 5 to 6 for medium. (Test the meat for doneness with an instant-read thermometer; it should read between 130°F and 135°F for medium-rare.) Remove the pan from the heat. Transfer the meat and the bacon-wrapped prunes to a large plate and allow to rest for 5 minutes.

To the pan, add the shallots and garlic and sauté for 2 minutes. Add the red wine, cassis and beef stock and reduce to a third, 4 to 5 minutes. Season to taste with salt and pepper. Place a fine-mesh sieve over a clean saucepan. Strain the sauce into the pan and discard the solids. Place the sauce over low heat and keep hot until needed.

Celeriac purée Melt the butter in a saucepan on medium heat, add the celeriac and cook until well coated with butter but not brown, 2 to 3 minutes. Add the milk and herbs, bring to a boil, then reduce the heat to medium-low and simmer for about 30 minutes until the celeriac is very tender. Drain the celeriac, reserving the milk but discarding the herbs.

Transfer the celeriac to a blender or food processor and blend until very smooth, adding enough of the reserved milk to give a creamy consistency. Season with salt and white pepper. Keep hot until needed.

To serve Ladle some of the celeriac purée into the middle of each plate and spread it into a circle. Thinly slice the venison on the diagonal, fold it and set it on the purée. Lean a chop against the sliced venison, top with 3 prunes each and serve immediately.

Venison chop

12 slices of double-smoked bacon

12 prunes, pitted

4 venison chops, each 5 oz

1 Tbsp vegetable oil

¼ c unsalted butter

1 shallot, in small dice

2 garlic cloves, minced

⅓ c red wine

3 Tbsp crème de cassis (blackcurrant liqueur)

⅓ c beef stock (page 173)

Celeriac purée

3 Tbsp butter

1 lb celeriac, peeled and chopped in 1-inch cubes

3½ c milk

1 small bay leaf

2 sprigs of thyme

white pepper

 CHEF'S NOTES Be sure not to overcook the venison, as this lean meat can become quite tough and gamey in flavour when cooked beyond medium.

Mix things up by replacing the celeriac with cauliflower or sweet potatoes.

Grilled Lamb Chops

WITH OLIVE TAPENADE HERB CRUST

Olive and sun-dried tomato tapenade Place the olives, sun-dried tomatoes and garlic in a small food processor and process until the mixture is smooth. With the motor running, slowly add the olive oil in a thin steady stream until the mixture forms a thick, smooth paste (adding the oil slowly prevents the tapenade from separating). Add the lemon juice and season with salt and pepper. Will keep refrigerated in an airtight container for up to 1 week.

Lamb chops Preheat a grill on high heat and the oven to 400°F. Season the lamb with salt and pepper, then place the chops on the grill and cook quickly on each side until slightly rare, about 1 minute per side.

Remove the lamb from the grill and spread one side of each chop with 1 Tbsp of the olive tapenade. Spread the tapenade evenly, then sprinkle ½ Tbsp of the herb panko mixture overtop. Set the lamb chops on a small baking tray and bake until the chops are cooked to your liking, 6 to 7 minutes for medium-rare or 7 to 8 minutes for medium. (To test for doneness, insert an instant-read thermometer into the thickest part of the meat; it should read between 130°F and 135°F for medium-rare.)

CHEF'S NOTE If you don't have the time to prepare the olive tapenade, use Dijon mustard as a tasty alternative.

Olive and sun-dried tomato tapenade

½ c kalamata olives, pitted

½ c sun-dried tomatoes in oil, drained

1 garlic clove, chopped

2 Tbsp extra-virgin olive oil

juice of ¼ lemon

Lamb chops

8 lamb chops, each 2 oz

4 Tbsp herb panko (page 92)

DESSERTS

Our version of an oldie-but-goodie is a Dirty Apron favourite, especially
with my five-year-old daughter, Chase. YIELDS 24 COOKIES

Oatmeal Raisin Cookies

1 c unsalted butter, room
temperature

1 c granulated sugar

1 c brown sugar

4 eggs

1 tsp vanilla extract

1½ c all-purpose flour

2 tsp baking soda

2 tsp baking powder

⅔ tsp salt

3⅓ c quick-cooking or rolled oats

2 c unsweetened shredded
coconut

1 c sultana raisins

Preheat the oven to 325°F. Line two baking sheets with parchment paper.

In a stand mixer fitted with a paddle attachment, cream the butter and both
sugars until well combined. Add the eggs and vanilla and mix to combine. Add the
flour, baking soda, baking powder and salt and mix just until a dough is formed.
Using a spatula, fold in the oats, coconut and raisins until they are evenly distributed.

Using an ice cream scoop, drop 24 spoonfuls of dough onto the baking sheets,
leaving 1½ to 2 inches between each one. Using wet hands, press the dough flat.
Bake for 6 minutes, then turn the baking sheet and bake until the cookies are golden,
5 to 6 minutes more. Remove from the oven, allow to cool slightly on the baking
sheets and then transfer to a wire rack.

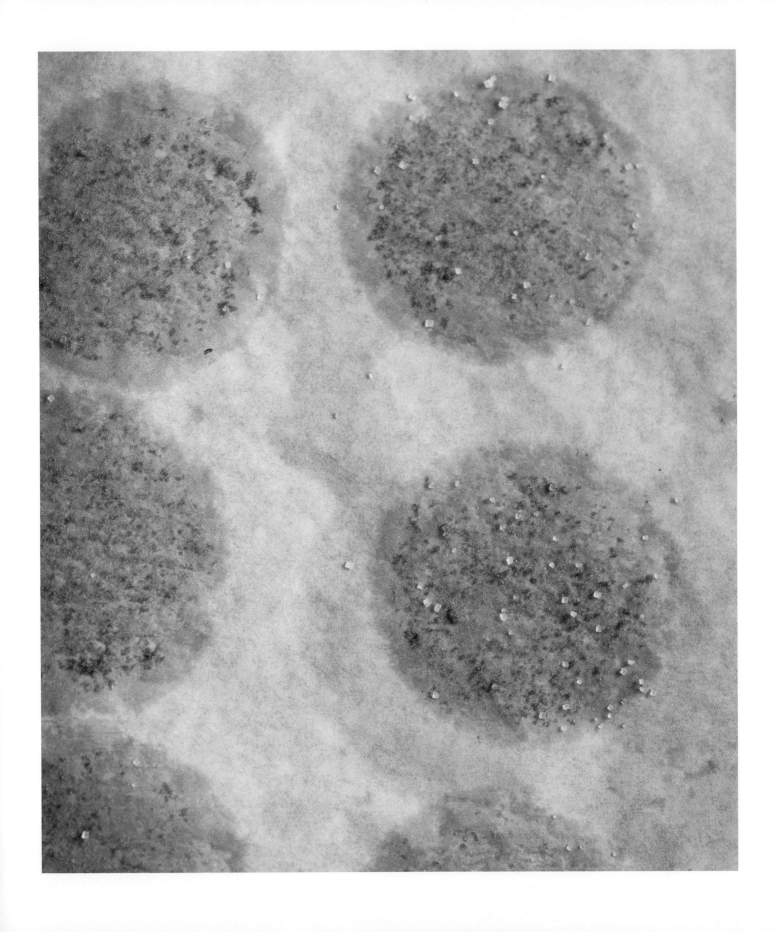

An extremely fudgy cookie that pleases all chocolate lovers. YIELDS 12 COOKIES

Double Chocolate Pecan Cookies

11 oz bittersweet chocolate

2½ Tbsp unsalted butter

3 eggs

¾ c granulated sugar

2 Tbsp + 1 tsp brewed coffee

2 tsp vanilla extract

⅔ c all-purpose flour

½ tsp baking powder

¼ tsp salt

36 whole pecans

white chocolate chips,
for garnish

Preheat the oven to 325°F. Line a baking sheet with parchment paper.

Melt the chocolate and butter in a small saucepan over low heat. Remove from the heat and set aside.

In a stand mixer fitted with a whisk attachment, beat the eggs and sugar until light in colour and tripled in volume, about 5 minutes. Add the coffee and vanilla, then the chocolate mixture. Sift in the flour, baking powder and salt and mix until the dough is uniform. Do not overmix.

Using an ice cream scoop, drop 12 mounds of dough onto the baking sheets, leaving 1½ to 2 inches between each one. Top each cookie with 3 pecans and some chocolate chips. Bake for 6 minutes, then turn the baking sheet and bake until the cookies are set, about 5 minutes. Remove from the oven, allow to cool slightly on the baking sheets and then transfer to a wire rack.

Biscotti are great because you always have the option of switching up different nuts and fruits and bringing different flavours into the recipe. In our classes, we set out a range of ingredients and allow students to add as many or as few as they like. Some of our most popular variations include white chocolate, macadamia nut and orange zest; dark chocolate, lemon zest and vanilla bean paste; and apricot and almond. The dough can be frozen ahead of time, too. At the Dirty Apron, we make batches of dough, freeze it and thaw as required. YIELDS 20 BISCOTTI

Italian Biscotti

Preheat the oven to 325°F. Line a baking sheet with parchment paper.

Place the butter and sugar in a medium bowl and beat together using a spatula or a wooden spoon. When the mixture is uniform and slightly fluffy, add the egg and keep mixing until it is combined.

In a small bowl, sift together the flour and baking powder (and any dry spices you might be using). Fold the flour mixture into the wet ingredients. Then fold in nuts, chocolate, zest, dried fruits and any extracts. Mix until just combined.

Using your hands, shape the batter into logs 1 inch thick and arrange them on the baking sheet. Brush each of the logs liberally with the beaten egg. Bake for 30 to 40 minutes, until light golden. Remove from the oven and reduce the temperature to 275°F. Allow the cookies to cool slightly.

Cut each log on the bias about 1 inch thick and return them to the baking sheet. Bake for another 30 minutes. Remove from the oven, allow to cool on the baking sheet then turn them out onto a wire rack. Will keep in an airtight container for 3 to 4 days.

⅓ c butter, softened

½ c sugar

1 egg

¾ c all-purpose flour

2 tsp baking powder

1 egg yolk mixed with a little water

Suggested additions

⅓ c chopped nuts

⅓ c finely chopped chocolate

zest of 1 orange

⅓ c chopped dried fruits

1 tsp vanilla extract

1 tsp cinnamon

 CHEF'S NOTE Biscotti are easy to make and adapt well to whatever additions you have on hand. We like to contrast sweet with salty, soft with crunchy, but experiment until you find your own favourites.

These humble bars are packed with lemon flavour. Finish them off with a light dusting of icing sugar, or pair them with glazed seasonal summer fruit or candied whole cranberries in the winter. This recipe makes a whole lot, so feel free to halve the recipe and bake it in a 9- × 13-inch pan (adjust the cooking times accordingly). Or cut into bars, pack into an airtight container or resealable plastic bags and freeze for up to 3 months. YIELDS 36 BARS

Lemon Bars

Shortbread base Preheat the oven to 325°F. Line a 12- × 16-inch half sheet pan that has a 1-inch rim with aluminum foil. Spray the pan with nonstick cooking spray and line it with parchment paper. Spray it with another layer of cooking spray. Set aside.

In the bowl of a stand mixer fitted with a paddle attachment, cream the butter and sugar until well combined. Add the vanilla and beat until well mixed. Add the flour and salt and mix just until combined. Press the shortbread dough evenly into the prepared pan, then prick it all over with a fork. Bake until set and lightly golden, about 20 minutes. Remove from the oven and set aside. Leave the oven on.

Lemon filling Place all the ingredients in a large bowl and whisk steadily until the mixture forms a smooth batter. Pour the filling over the hot shortbread base and bake until set, about 30 minutes. (The filling is set when it jiggles like jelly.) Allow to cool before cutting into individual bars.

  CHEF'S NOTE Prepare the filling while the shortbread base is cooking.

Shortbread base

2 c unsalted butter, room temperature

1 c granulated sugar

1 Tbsp vanilla paste or ½ Tbsp vanilla extract

4 c all-purpose flour

1 tsp salt

Lemon filling

14 eggs

5 c granulated sugar

¼ c lemon zest

2 c lemon juice

2 c all-purpose flour

143

This dessert is a hybrid of my two favourite chocolate bars, Twix and Skor. These are sinfully rich bars that showcase our shortbread, a dulce de leche centre and salted caramel ganache. Make sure to sprinkle a thin line of fleur de sel on top to make this an extra-special indulgence. This recipe makes a lot of bars. You can either halve the recipe and cook the Dirty Twixters in a 9- × 13-inch pan or cut them into squares, seal into an airtight container or plastic bags, and refrigerate for up to 1 week. YIFLDS 36 BARS

The Dirty Twixter Bars

Brown sugar shortbread base

1 c brown sugar

3½ c all-purpose flour

1 Tbsp vanilla paste

2 c unsalted butter, in small cubes

Dulce de leche filling

2 cans (each 12 oz) sweetened condensed milk

1 tsp fleur de sel

Salted caramel ganache

9 oz bittersweet chocolate, roughly chopped

1 lb 2½ oz milk chocolate, roughly chopped

1 c unsalted butter

2¼ c whipping cream

2½ c granulated sugar

⅔ c water

2½ tsp fleur de sel

2 tsp vanilla paste

Brown sugar shortbread base Preheat the oven to 350°F. Line a 12- × 16-inch half sheet pan that has a 1-inch rim with aluminum foil. Spray the pan with nonstick cooking spray and line it with parchment paper. Set aside.

In the bowl of a stand mixer fitted with a paddle attachment, mix the brown sugar and flour until combined. Add the vanilla and beat until well mixed. Slowly add the butter, one cube at a time, and beat at medium-low until the dough is just combined. Press the shortbread dough evenly into the prepared pan, then prick it all over with a fork. Bake for about 25 minutes, or until set and lightly golden. Remove from the oven and allow to cool.

Dulce de leche filling Place the cans in a pot large enough to cover them with 4 inches of water. Add the water, bring to a boil on high heat and cook, uncovered, for 4 hours, checking occasionally to be sure the water is still covering the cans. (Add more water, if necessary, to be sure the cans are constantly covered with water.) Turn off the heat and set aside, leaving the cans in the water until everything comes to room temperature.

Open the cans and spoon the sticky brown dulce de leche into a bowl. Using a spoon, stir until the mixture is smooth, then spread it over the shortbread base. Sprinkle evenly with fleur de sel. Set aside.

Salted caramel ganache Place the dark and milk chocolates in a large heatproof bowl and set aside. Combine the butter and cream in a small pot over low heat and cook until warm to the touch. Remove from the heat and set aside.

Heat the sugar and water in a large pot over high heat and boil the mixture, without stirring, until it reaches 250°F. (Use a candy thermometer to test the temperature.) Slowly pour the cream mixture into this syrup to make a caramel. Stir in the fleur de sel and vanilla, then pour the salted caramel over the combined chocolates and allow to sit for 5 minutes. Using a handheld blender, emulsify the mixture to make a ganache. Avoid making large bubbles. Pour this ganache over the dulce de leche and refrigerate the bars overnight. Cut into individual bars before serving.

This is our signature bar. We bake these brownies gluten-free for our deli by substituting an all-purpose gluten-free flour mix. Be patient when whipping your eggs—that's the secret to the creamy texture of the filling. These brownies won't last long, but you can halve the recipe and bake them in a 9- × 13-inch pan (adjust the cooking time accordingly) or freeze leftovers in an airtight container or resealable plastic bags for up to 3 months. YIELDS 36 BARS

Pistachio Cream Cheese Brownies

Pistachio cream cheese In the bowl of a stand mixer fitted with a paddle attachment, beat all the ingredients at high speed until smooth. Set aside.

Brownie base Preheat the oven to 325°F. Line a 12- × 16-inch half sheet pan that has a 1-inch rim with aluminum foil. Spray the pan with nonstick cooking spray and line it with parchment paper. Spray it with another layer of nonstick cooking spray. Set aside. Sift the flour and cocoa together into a small bowl and set aside.

Melt the butter and chocolate in a small pot over low heat, then remove from the heat and set aside.

In the bowl of a stand mixer fitted with a whisk attachment, whisk the sugar and eggs until very light in colour and tripled in volume. Slowly drizzle in the chocolate mixture, then scrape down the bowl with a spatula and whisk until uniformly combined. Slowly sift in the dry ingredients and whisk until just combined. Spread the brownie base evenly into the prepared pan.

Spoon the pistachio cream cheese into a pastry bag fitted with a round tip and pipe 7 evenly spaced lines lengthwise over the brownie base. Drag a small knife from side to side through the batter and the cream cheese in even intervals to form a pattern. Bake until set and a small knife inserted in the dough releases only wet crumbs, about 25 minutes. Remove from the oven, allow to cool and then cut into bars.

Pistachio cream cheese

1 c cream cheese

⅓ c granulated sugar

2 oz pistachio paste
(see Chef's Note)

1 Tbsp whipping cream

Brownie base

1⅓ c all-purpose flour

1 c cocoa

1½ c unsalted butter

12 oz bittersweet
chocolate, roughly chopped

2⅔ c granulated sugar

6 eggs

CHEF'S NOTE We use pure nut pastes to make our desserts. They can be expensive, but the flavour is worth it. Look for pistachio paste in specialty food stores or make your own in a spice grinder by grinding 8¾ oz unsalted shelled pistachios with 3½ oz of granulated sugar and just enough water (no more than 1 oz) to make a paste with the consistency of thick peanut butter.

When Portuguese labourers from Madeira and the Azores came to Hawaii in the late nineteenth century, they brought this home-style deep-fried pastry with them. We use their malasada-style recipe here. This doughnut is a regular feature on the Dirty Apron "Deep Frydays" menu, and it forms the base for the Yuzu Curd Dirty Doughnut and the Maple Bacon Dirty Doughnuts below. This recipe makes a lot of doughnuts, especially when you make mini doughnuts (about ½ oz) as we do at the Dirty Apron. You can make yours regular size (1½ to 2 oz) or halve the recipe. Or make the dough, divide it in three and make some of each variation. YIELDS 6 LB OF DOUGH (ABOUT 135 MINI DOUGHNUTS OR 45 REGULAR-SIZE ONES)

The Dirty Doughnuts

Doughnut glaze Combine the butter, sugar and vanilla in a medium bowl. Slowly add the water, whisking, until the glaze is thin but still sticky enough to adhere to the doughnut in a transparent coat. Set aside at room temperature.

Basic Dirty Doughnut dough To make the sponge, stir together 4 cups of the flour and the yeast in a large bowl. Pour in the milk and water, stirring just until all the flour is moistened. Cover the bowl with plastic wrap and set it aside in a warm place for about 20 minutes, or until the sponge appears light and bubbly and rises and falls when you tap the bowl.

Lightly grease a large bowl with vegetable oil. In a stand mixer with a dough hook attachment, combine the sponge, sugar, salt, eggs, butter and the remaining flour and knead until the dough windowpanes (page 18) when stretched. Place the dough in the oiled bowl and cover it with plastic wrap. Allow the dough to rise until it has doubled in size, about 1 hour.

Lightly dust a clean work surface with flour. Roll out the dough to a thickness of ¼ inch and cut it into your favourite doughnut shapes. Allow the cut doughnuts to rise and rest for 20 minutes, or until doubled in size.

Set a wire rack on a baking sheet. Fill a deep fryer or a deep-sided pot ⅔ full with oil and heat to 350°F. (Use a deep-fat thermometer to test the temperature.) Carefully drop the doughnuts (in batches, if necessary) into the oil and cook until they are golden and reach an internal temperature of 195°F, about 3 minutes per side for the minis, or 4 minutes for the regular size. Using tongs, transfer the cooked doughnuts to the wire rack to drain for 1 minute.

Roll the warm doughnuts in the glaze, ensuring they are completely covered, then return them to the wire rack until you are ready to serve them.

Doughnut glaze

⅔ c melted unsalted butter

4 c icing sugar

1 Tbsp vanilla extract

½ c water, boiling

Basic Dirty Doughnut dough

9½ c all-purpose flour

1 Tbsp + 1 tsp instant yeast

2¾ c milk (90°F–95°F)

½ c water (90°F–95°F)

vegetable oil

1 c sugar

1¼ tsp salt

4 eggs

⅔ c butter, room temperature

Yuzu curd

8 egg yolks

1 c granulated sugar

½ c yuzu juice (or citrus juice or passionfruit purée)

¾ c unsalted butter, cold, in small cubes

1 recipe cooked Dirty Doughnuts, unglazed

icing sugar, for dusting

Candied bacon

2¼ lbs bacon, in ¼-inch dice

1 c brown sugar

1 Tbsp cinnamon

1 recipe basic Dirty Doughnut dough, unrisen

maple syrup to glaze

VARIATION: THE YUZU CURD DIRTY DOUGHNUT

Yuzu curd Set a stainless steel bowl over a pot filled with water and bring it to a simmer over medium-low heat.

Combine the egg yolks, granulated sugar and yuzu juice in the bowl and cook, stirring constantly with a heat-resistant spatula, until the mixture coats the back of a spoon and reaches 160°F. (Test the temperature with an instant-read thermometer.)

Remove the bowl from the heat and add the butter, one cube at a time, stirring until smooth. Transfer the curd to a bowl, cover it tightly with plastic wrap—pressing the wrap directly on to the surface of the curd to prevent it from forming a skin—and refrigerate until chilled and set, ideally overnight.

To assemble Once the doughnuts have cooled to room temperature, fill a pastry bag with the yuzu curd. Attach a plain round tip, insert the tip into the side of each doughnut and fill it until it feels heavy for its size. Place the icing sugar in a shallow bowl, then dip the doughnuts in the sugar before serving.

VARIATION: THE MAPLE BACON DIRTY DOUGHNUT

Candied bacon Preheat the oven to 350°F. Line a baking sheet with parchment paper.

Combine the bacon, brown sugar and cinnamon in a large bowl, stirring well to ensure the bacon is evenly coated. Arrange the bacon in a single layer on the baking sheet and bake until crispy and bubbly, about 20 minutes. Remove from the oven and set aside to cool.

To assemble Add the bacon to the basic doughnut recipe before allowing it to rise. Cut, rest and fry the doughnuts as usual, then roll in the maple syrup before serving.

CHEF'S NOTE Look for yuzu juice at Asian food markets. If you can't find it, a combination of lemon and orange juice—or any other citrus juice—makes a good substitute.

THE DIRTY APRON DESSERT PHILOSOPHY

I'll be totally honest. I'm not a dessert kind of chef. If I had my way, I'd finish a meal with some fine cheeses and fruit. Which is not to say that I don't appreciate a delectable dessert—or the ideas behind it. In high school, I loved the science of cooking, and I knew that too much baking powder in a muffin would make it explode. So in home economics class, I sabotaged everyone's muffin batter and, when the muffins started exploding inside the ovens, got myself kicked out of class. Ironically, the teacher, Mrs. Mah, told me that I'd never have a future as a chef…

Today, I still love the ideas behind dessert, but I'm mostly focused on the flavours and textures. At the Dirty Apron, we take a simple, thematic approach to our desserts. The ingredients are unified by the familiar, but made new. Most of us have a particular dessert that brings up memories of our childhood, when mom was rolling out the dough in the kitchen or letting us lick the icing off the wooden spoon. At Dirty Apron, many of our desserts are inspired by those comfort foods. I work closely with our pastry chef, Kat. I can convey my ideas, and she develops them into the types of desserts our customers will come back for. Take the Dirty Twixter Bars (page 144)—we retain the familiar flavour from the chocolate bars but elevate the ingredients.

When planning your own desserts, work around a theme so all the components come together on the plate. For example, I've long believed that the ideal dessert has a hot and cold component, which is why the whole world loves hot apple pie with ice cream. You've got a lot of dynamics in that classic: the heat, the cold, the soft and crispy textures, the tartness, the sweetness, a little saltiness from the crust. Using versatile ingredients, such as puff pastry and crêpes that can be made ahead and used with sweet or savoury fillings, is often a good start. And keep the plate simple, not complicated. Use fresh high-quality ingredients and let them sing as they are.

This sorbet is a great finish to our San Sebastián cooking class. It's inspired by all the usual suspects found in a Spanish sangria—red wine, chopped fruits, a sweetener and a small amount of brandy. YIELDS 7 CUPS (SERVES 14)

Sangria Sorbet

1 bottle (750 mL) red wine

1 can (330 mL)
San Pellegrino limonata

1 can (330 mL)
San Pellegrino aranciata

1 large orange, cut into rings

1 large lemon, cut into rings

1 large lime, cut into rings

1 c granulated sugar

½ c Grand Marnier

Coconut lime sorbet

2 c coconut milk

2 c cream of coconut

1 c fresh lime juice

1 c granulated sugar

½ c water

1 vanilla bean, split lengthwise
and seeds reserved

fine zest of 2 limes

Combine the red wine, limonata, aranciata, fruits and sugar in a large non-reactive pot and bring to a boil over high heat. Reduce the heat to low and simmer for 5 minutes. Remove from the heat. Set a fine-mesh sieve over a non-reactive bowl, and strain the sangria through it. Discard the solids. Stir in the Grand Marnier and refrigerate the mixture until cool, about 2 hours. Pour the sorbet base into the ice cream maker and process according to the manufacturer's instructions. Will keep frozen in the ice cream maker or an airtight container for up to 3 months.

VARIATION: COCONUT LIME SORBET

Coconut milk is the rich creamy liquid made from water and coconut pulp pressed out from the thick white flesh of matured coconuts. Cream of coconut is a delicious cream made from coconut milk blended with cane sugar. This sorbet uses both, and although it's vegan, it's just as rich as ice cream. We finish our Thai cooking class with this dessert. YIELDS 6 CUPS (SERVES 12)

Have ready an ice cream maker.

Place the coconut milk, cream of coconut and lime juice in a large heatproof bowl and set aside.

Bring the sugar, water, vanilla bean and seeds, and lime zest to a boil in a small pot over high heat. Pour the vanilla syrup into the coconut-lime mixture, stir to combine and refrigerate until cool. Remove and discard the vanilla bean. Pour the sorbet base into the ice cream maker and proceed according to the manufacturer's instructions. Will keep frozen in the ice cream maker or an airtight container for up to 3 months.

 CHEF'S NOTE If you don't have cream of coconut, substitute the top layer from a can of full-fat coconut milk that has been refrigerated overnight then neither shaken nor stirred, or use 1 cup of whipping cream + ½ cup coconut cream powder. Add sugar to taste.

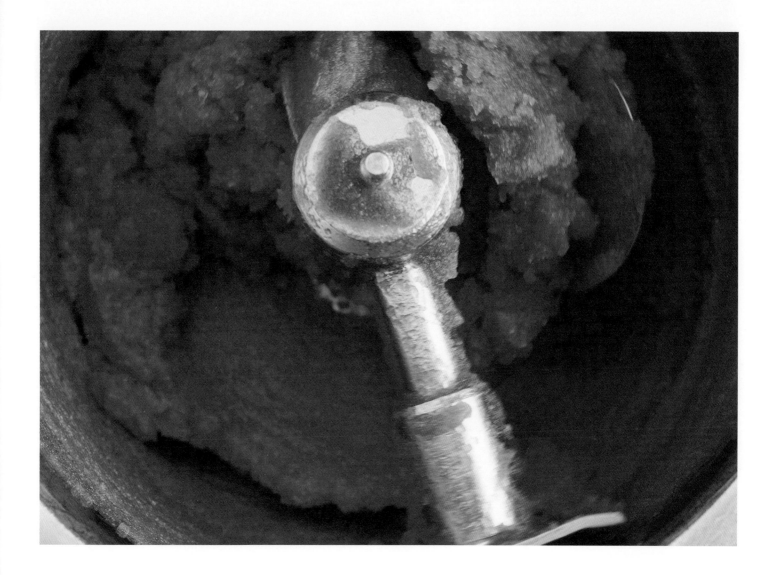

VARIATION: CHAMPAGNE SORBET

We finish off our Summer in the City cooking class with this decadent sorbet. True champagne is the sparkling wine produced from grapes that are grown in France's Champagne region. We use real champagne here, no substitutes. YIELDS 10 CUPS (SERVES 20)

Combine the sugar, water, orange zest, and vanilla bean and seeds in a small pot over high heat and bring to a boil. Remove from the heat and refrigerate until cool. Set a fine-mesh sieve over a non-reactive bowl, and strain the flavoured syrup through it. Discard the solids. Stir in the champagne, then pour the mixture into an ice cream maker and process according to the manufacturer's instructions. Will keep frozen in the ice cream maker or an airtight container for up to 3 months.

Champagne sorbet

1⅓ c granulated sugar

1 c water

zest of 2 large oranges, in 1-inch strips

1 vanilla bean, split lengthwise and seeds reserved

1 bottle (750 mL) champagne

155

What is French vanilla ice cream but a frozen crème anglaise? This recipe is our house vanilla ice cream and also the base for the Pistachio Ice Cream from our La Cucina Toscana cooking class. We also use it as the base for our Bourbon Ice Cream and Kahlúa Ice Cream. Start this recipe a couple of days before you plan to serve it. Will keep frozen in an airtight container for up to 3 months. YIELDS 4 CUPS (SERVES 8)

French Vanilla Ice Cream

1½ c whole milk

2 c whipping cream

⅔ c granulated sugar

1 generous Tbsp glucose syrup or light corn syrup

1 vanilla bean, split lengthwise and seeds reserved

12 egg yolks

Pistachio ice cream

4 oz pistachio paste (page 147)

1 c pistachios, toasted and chopped

Bourbon ice cream

⅔ c demerara sugar

⅓ c good-quality bourbon

Kahlúa ice cream

⅔ c demerara sugar

1 heaping Tbsp ground coffee

⅓ c Kahlúa

French vanilla ice cream base Combine the milk, cream, ⅓ cup of the sugar, the glucose (or corn syrup), and the vanilla bean and seeds in a medium saucepan over medium-high heat. Heat until hot but do not allow the mixture to simmer. Remove from the heat and allow to steep for 30 minutes.

In the bowl of a stand mixer fitted with a whisk attachment, add the egg yolks and the remaining sugar and beat at high speed until light in colour and tripled in volume, about 3 minutes. Reduce the speed to medium and add 1 cup of the milk mixture. Beat until combined, then add a second cup of the milk mixture. Turn off the mixer and pour the egg mixture into the saucepan.

Cook the ice cream base over medium heat, stirring constantly with a heat-resistant spatula, until it coats the back of the spatula and reaches 180°F. (Test the temperature with an instant-read thermometer.)

Set a stainless steel bowl in a roasting pan filled with ice. Place a fine-mesh sieve over the bowl. Strain the mixture through the sieve and discard any solids. Allow the mixture to cool over the ice, stirring often. Cover the bowl with plastic wrap and refrigerate overnight.

Pour the mixture into an ice cream maker and process according to the manufacturer's instructions.

VARIATIONS

Pistachio ice cream Follow the instructions for the French vanilla ice cream base, heating the pistachio paste along with the milk mixture. Fold in the pistachios after straining the ice cream base.

Bourbon ice cream Follow the instructions for the French vanilla ice cream base, substituting demerara sugar for granulated sugar and adding the bourbon just before pouring the mixture into the ice cream maker.

Kahlúa ice cream Follow the instructions for the French vanilla ice cream base, substituting demerara sugar for granulated sugar and heating the coffee along with the milk mixture. Add the Kahlúa just before pouring the mixture into the ice cream maker.

This ice cream base uses the flambé cooking technique, which is easy, even for the home cook. For safety's sake, be sure to remove the pan from the heat before adding the Calvados. Start this ice cream a couple of days before you plan to serve it. YIELDS 4 CUPS (SERVES 8)

Calvados Apple Ice Cream

Melt the butter in a large sauté pan over medium heat. Add ½ cup of the sugar, whisk until emulsified and then cook until thick and bubbly, about 3 minutes. Remove the pan from the heat, add the Calvados, then using a barbecue lighter or a long match, carefully ignite the alcohol. Allow the flames to burn out, then whisk the mixture vigorously, add the apples and, using a heat-resistant spatula, toss them gently until well coated. Stir in the cinnamon, return the pan to medium-low heat and cook until the apples are tender, about 3 minutes. Transfer the apple mixture to a blender or food processor and purée until smooth, then refrigerate until cool, about 20 minutes.

Combine the milk, cream, ¼ cup of the sugar, the glucose (or corn syrup), and the vanilla bean and seeds in a medium saucepan over medium-high heat. Heat until hot but do not allow the mixture to simmer. Remove from the heat and allow to steep for 30 minutes.

In the bowl of a stand mixer fitted with a whisk attachment, add the egg yolks and the remaining sugar and beat at high speed until light in colour and tripled in volume, about 3 minutes. Reduce the speed to medium and add 1 cup of the milk mixture. Beat until combined, then add a second cup of the milk mixture. Turn off the mixer and pour the egg mixture into the saucepan.

Cook the ice cream base over medium heat, stirring constantly with a heat-resistant spatula, until it coats the back of the spatula and reaches 180°F. (Test the temperature with an instant-read thermometer.)

Set a stainless steel bowl in a roasting pan filled with ice. Place a fine-mesh sieve over the bowl. Strain the mixture through the sieve and discard any solids. Add the reserved apple purée and stir until well combined. Allow the mixture to cool over the ice bath, stirring often. Cover the bowl with plastic wrap and refrigerate overnight.

Pour the mixture into an ice cream maker and process according to the manufacturer's instructions.

⅓ c unsalted butter

1 c demerara sugar

⅓ c Calvados (apple brandy)

3 large Granny Smith apples, peeled, cored and thinly sliced

1 Tbsp cinnamon

1 c whole milk

2 c whipping cream

1 generous Tbsp glucose syrup or light corn syrup

¼ tsp salt

1 vanilla bean, split lengthwise and seeds reserved

6 egg yolks

I teach this dessert in my Italian class. It's the Italian version of a French crème brûlée, but without the caramelized sugar on top. You can make it a day ahead. The key to this recipe is making sure that you add the gelatin to the liquid while it's still hot, and that you whisk thoroughly for a good 45 seconds to one minute. If you don't follow these rules, your panna cotta won't set and it will come out too loose. SERVES 4

Lemon Panna Cotta

Candied lemon zest Using a vegetable peeler, remove all the zest from the lemon. Finely julienne the zest into long strips.

Combine the water and sugar in a small pot and bring it to a boil over high heat. Add the lemon zest, reduce the heat to medium and simmer until tender, about 20 minutes.

Preheat the oven to 220°F. Line a baking sheet with parchment paper. Drain the zest in a colander, then arrange it, loosely separating each strand, on the baking sheet. Sprinkle with granulated sugar until lightly coated and bake on the middle rack for about 20 minutes or until crisp. Remove from the oven, allow to cool and separate into individual strands.

Lemon panna cotta Chill four 3-inch ramekins or bowls. Combine the cream, sugar and lemon zest in a saucepan over medium-high heat and, stirring gently, bring to a boil. Remove from the heat and whisk in the gelatin until it dissolves, for a good minute.

Set a fine-mesh sieve over a bowl, then strain the cream mixture into it. Discard the solids. Stir the milk into the cream mixture, then pour it into the ramekins (or bowls). Refrigerate for at least 2 hours before serving, so it has time to set.

Serve each panna cotta chilled with a few strands of candied lemon zest.

CHEF'S NOTES Candied lemon zest will keep in an airtight container for up to 3 days.

Make sure the cream mixture is hot before you add the gelatin, so the gelatin can dissolve properly.

Candied lemon zest

2 lemons

1 c water

1 c granulated sugar + more for sprinkling

Lemon panna cotta

1¾ c whipping cream

⅓ c granulated sugar

zest of 2 lemons

1 Tbsp powdered gelatin

½ c whole milk

What's good about this soufflé recipe is you can make it ahead of time, put the batter into moulds and let it rise later. It's flourless, so the flour doesn't bog it down while it's sitting. Once it rises in the oven, you have a minute before it goes back down, so you might want to take a picture. In class, I usually hold a competition to see whose soufflé rises the highest. SERVES 4

Orange and Cinnamon Chocolate Soufflés

WITH CHOCOLATE SAUCE

Orange and cinnamon chocolate soufflés

½ c dark chocolate (70% cocoa)

zest of 1 orange

¼ c butter + more, softened, for brushing the moulds

4 egg whites

¼ c granulated sugar + more for the moulds

1 Tbsp cinnamon

4 egg yolks

icing sugar

Chocolate sauce

½ c water

2 Tbsp granulated sugar

¼ c cocoa powder

⅓ c dark chocolate (70% cocoa), chopped

Orange and cinnamon chocolate soufflés Preheat the oven to 400°F. Prepare four 3-inch soufflé moulds by brushing the insides with butter then refrigerating them until the butter is set, about 5 minutes. Remove the moulds from the fridge, repeat with another layer of butter, then sprinkle with sugar and tap out the excess. Refrigerate until needed.

In the top of a double boiler placed over medium heat, melt the chocolate, orange zest and butter. Remove from the heat and set aside.

Place the egg whites in a large bowl and, using a handheld mixer, beat at high speed until they form soft peaks, about 3 minutes. With the motor running, slowly add the sugar, beating until the egg whites are stiff and glossy, about 1 minute more.

Stir the cinnamon into the melted chocolate, wait about 1 minute, then beat in the egg yolks all at once. Using a spatula, gently fold this mixture into the egg whites until it is a uniform colour. Spoon the batter into a piping bag fitted with a round tip and pipe enough batter to reach ¼ inch below the top of each mould. Place the soufflé dishes on a baking sheet and bake for about 12 minutes. (They will still be moist when ready.) Arrange the soufflés on individual plates and dust with icing sugar.

Chocolate sauce Bring the water, sugar and cocoa powder to a boil in a small pot on low heat. Add the chocolate, remove from the heat and stir until the chocolate has melted and the sauce is smooth.

To serve Serve the soufflés on individual plates with a bowl of the chocolate sauce alongside. Just before serving, use a spoon to crack open the top of each soufflé and pour in some of the hot chocolate sauce.

 CHEF'S NOTE Before you make the soufflés, start the chocolate sauce. Serve the soufflés as soon as they come out of the oven, as they will start to sink shortly after.

One afternoon we asked our followers on Twitter to tell us their favourite comfort dessert. We then chose one to make in class. The winner was a sticky toffee pudding, which we elevated by adding Bailey's to the sauce, in honour of my mother, who is Irish. Serve with your favourite ice cream, such as the Calvados Apple Ice Cream (page 157). SERVES 4

Sticky Toffee Puddings

WITH BAILEY'S CARAMEL SAUCE

Sticky toffee puddings Preheat the oven to 350°F. Butter 4 cups in a muffin tin.

Place the dates, coffee and water in a small saucepan and bring to a boil over medium heat. Cook, stirring often, for 2 minutes, then remove from the heat, stir in the baking soda and allow to sit for 5 minutes.

Stir together the flour and baking powder in a small bowl. Place the butter, sugar and eggs in a medium bowl and beat together until well combined. Beat in the flour mixture, then stir in the dates. Spoon enough batter into each muffin cup to fill it ½ full.

Bring a large kettle of water to a boil. Set the muffin tin into a large roasting pan. Fill the roasting pan half full of water, so it reaches halfway up the sides of the muffin tin. Bake on the middle rack for 15 minutes. Reduce the heat to 325°F, then continue baking until a skewer inserted in the centre of the puddings comes out clean, about 15 minutes. Remove the roasting pan from the oven and transfer the muffin tin to a wire rack to cool. Run a knife along the inside edges of the muffin tins to unmould the puddings.

Bailey's caramel sauce Melt the butter and brown sugar in a small pan over medium heat. Stir in the cream and Irish cream and allow to boil gently until slightly thickened, about 2 minutes.

To serve Place the puddings on individual plates with generous lashings of hot caramel sauce.

Sticky toffee puddings

1 c dates, pitted and coarsely chopped

2 tsp instant coffee granules

½ c water

1 tsp baking soda

¾ c all-purpose flour

1 tsp baking powder

2 Tbsp unsalted butter, room temperature + more, softened, for brushing the muffin tins

¼ c granulated sugar

2 eggs, beaten

Bailey's caramel sauce

3 Tbsp unsalted butter

⅓ c brown sugar, lightly packed

3 Tbsp whipping cream

2 Tbsp Bailey's Irish cream

This recipe is a beauty. I was inspired to poach the pears in the syrup from a spiced wine I've had while on our trips to Germany at Christmas, and the cooked pears are so good on their own you can make them without the pastry. Just serve them with ice cream for a delicious, relatively easy and elegant dessert. If you make the tarts, garnish each one with a spoonful of mascarpone cheese and crushed hazelnuts. SERVES 4

Pear Tarts

WITH MUSCAT SABAYON

Poached pears and Muscat sabayon

½ c Frangelico liqueur

1½ c dry red wine

¼ c granulated sugar

1 vanilla bean, split lengthwise and seeds reserved

2 whole star anise

2 Bosc pears, each cut into 12 wedges

2 egg yolks

2 Tbsp Muscat

Roasted pear tarts

1 recipe rough or classic puff pastry (pages 178 and 177)

¼ c + 1 Tbsp butter, room temperature, in cubes

¼ c granulated sugar

1 egg

½ c ground almonds

2 Tbsp all-purpose flour

icing sugar

Poached pears and Muscat sabayon Place the Frangelico, red wine, sugar, vanilla bean and seeds, star anise and pears in a small saucepan over medium-high heat and simmer until reduced by half, 8 to 10 minutes. Remove from the heat and allow the pears and liquid to cool to room temperature, about 15 minutes. Using a slotted spoon, transfer the pears to a small bowl and set aside. Reserve the poaching liquid.

Set a stainless steel bowl over a small pot of simmering water on low heat. Place the egg yolks, ¼ cup of the reserved poaching liquid and the Muscat in the bowl and whisk continuously until the mixture is thick and has doubled in volume. Remove from the heat, cover and set aside. (Use the leftover poaching liquid as a syrup over other desserts or yoghurt.)

Roasted pear tarts Lightly dust a clean work surface with flour. Roll out the puff pastry to a square 25 inches across and ⅛ inch thick, transfer to a baking sheet and refrigerate for at least 5 minutes.

Prepare the frangipane by placing the ¼ cup of butter and the granulated sugar in a food processor. Process until pale and well combined. Add the egg, ground almonds and flour and process until uniform and well mixed.

Preheat the oven to 425°F. Line a baking sheet with a silicone mat (or parchment paper). Lightly dust a work surface with flour. Place the puff pastry on the counter and, using a saucer or a small plate, cut four 5-inch circles of pastry. Place the pastry circles on the baking sheet and prick them evenly with a fork. Spread a thin layer of the frangipane over each pastry round, leaving a ½-inch gap around the edges. Arrange the cooked pear wedges in a fan on top of the frangipane. Dot the tablespoon of butter cubes over the tarts and dust heavily with icing sugar. Bake for 12 minutes or until the pastry is crisp and the pears have caramelized slightly.

Serve the tarts warm on individual plates, drizzled with Muscat sabayon.

 CHEF'S NOTES Whisking continuously is important to prevent the egg from cooking in the bowl. If the egg starts to cook while you are whisking, reduce the heat or remove the sauce from the heat and allow the water to cool down.

If the tarts are not browned after 12 minutes, give them a couple more minutes to ensure a nice colour.

These tarts require a little more technique, so don't attempt them for the first time just before a big dinner party. But once you've mastered the art of making a curd, you'll keep making these little gems. The creamy sweet mango-and-citrus blend with the crispy crust of the tart is sublime. SERVES 4

Mango Lime Tarts

Almond crust

1 c all-purpose flour

½ c butter, cold

3 Tbsp icing sugar

2 Tbsp ground almonds

zest of 1 lemon

Mango curd

1½ c mango purée (about 2 large mangoes, roughly chopped and puréed until smooth)

½ c whipping cream

⅓ c granulated sugar

juice and zest of 1 lime

1 egg yolk

1 egg

1 Tbsp butter

1 mango, sliced (to garnish)

Almond crust Have ready four 5-inch tart pans, some baking weights (or dry beans) and two large sheets of parchment paper.

Place the flour, butter, icing sugar, almonds and lemon zest in a food processor fitted with a metal blade. Pulse the machine 8 to 10 times to break up the butter, then process until the dough forms a ball on one side of the bowl. Wrap in plastic wrap and refrigerate for 15 minutes.

Preheat the oven to 375°F. Place the dough between the sheets of parchment paper and roll it out to a thickness of ⅛ inch. Divide it into 4 pieces, then set the pastry over the tart pans and press the dough down into them, making sure to form it completely. Cut off the excess edges and refrigerate the pastry for 15 minutes.

To blind bake the tarts, prick the pastry with a fork, line it with parchment paper and fill it with the baking weights or dried beans. Bake for 10 minutes, then remove the weights (or beans) and bake for another 10 minutes. Remove from the oven and set aside.

Mango curd Place the mango purée, cream, sugar, lime juice and zest in a small pot over medium-low heat and bring to just below the boil.

Whisk together the egg yolk and the whole egg in a medium bowl. Add about ¼ cup of the mango mixture to the eggs and whisk well to temper the eggs. Add more of the mango mixture, ¼ cup at a time, until about half of it has been incorporated into the eggs.

Reduce the heat to low, then pour the tempered egg mixture into the pot and whisk until the curd reaches the ribbon stage, about 5 minutes. (The curd will stick to the back of the spoon.) Whisk in the butter.

To assemble Pour the mango curd into the prebaked tart shells and garnish with mango slices. Refrigerate for 25 minutes before serving.

 CHEF'S NOTE This recipe involves making and rolling pastry, blind baking and tempering eggs, so make sure you're not rushed when trying this recipe for the first time.

Gluten-Free Orange Almond Cakes

Preheat the oven to 325°F. Butter ten 2-inch cake moulds.

Combine all the ingredients in a large bowl, mixing them with a large spoon until just moistened. Divide the batter among the moulds and bake until the tops are golden and a small knife inserted into the cakes comes out clean, about 30 minutes.

CHEF'S NOTE To prepare ground oranges, wash the whole oranges and place them in a large pot filled with water. Boil over high heat until a knife inserted into an orange moves with ease, about 30 minutes. Transfer the oranges, peels and all, to a blender or food processor and process until smooth.

2 to 3 oranges, ground (see Chef's Note)

2¼ c ground almonds

1½ c granulated sugar

1 tsp baking powder

5 eggs

1 Tbsp vanilla paste

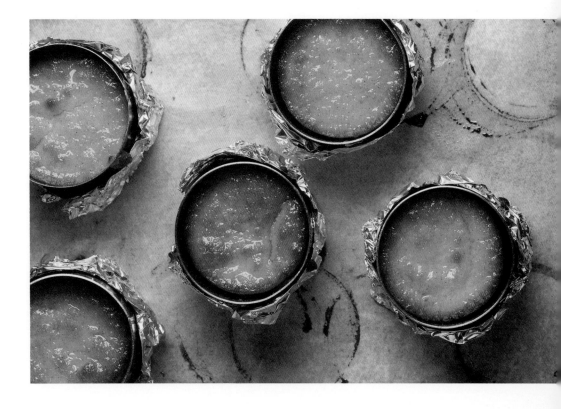

HOW TO PLAN A MENU

Menu planning is one of the most exciting jobs for a chef. It's the chance to put our creativity to the test, to challenge ourselves to go beyond our cooking routines. We have a regular customer at Dirty Apron Catering who each month orders a menu that is based on different countries for a large group of people. We've put together Moroccan, Japanese, Greek, Belgian menus for them. I'm not sure if they spin the globe to figure out what menu they want next, but I just know that they're having a lot of fun with it. It's a lot of fun for me to plan, too.

At home, you usually plan a three-course menu, but it's not unusual for professional chefs to plan up to ten or twelve courses. There is an art to menu planning, because you have to balance portion sizes as well as flavours. Pretend you're the guest and imagine what the meal experience will be like as you are served each course. That's the best way to pull off a successful menu.

Here are some tips:

- Write your menu down. It's always easier to see the flavours in each dish when you write out each course and the ingredients.

- Think about what food you want to showcase, keeping the season and freshness in mind. If it's spot prawn season, for example, let that be your inspiration. Make the prawns the star of the main course.

- Start with something light as an appetizer course, especially if your main is going to be rich. In the winter, I usually do a warm starter, such as a soup, and in summer, a cold dish, such as a salad or ceviche.

- Be keenly aware of strong flavours and use them judiciously. Nobody wants truffle oil drizzled over everything.

- Don't be redundant. You might love lemon, but it shouldn't be showcased in every course.

- It's not a hard-and-fast rule, but try to stick to themes when planning your menu. For example, I would never do an Italian meal and finish with a green tea crème brûlée. I would finish with an Italian panna cotta. Your menu should make sense.

- Balance the richness between dishes. If you served a main dish rich in butter and cream, for example, finish with a sorbet or other light dessert. And if you served a nice light fish main, then go for a decadent chocolate dessert.

- Do not overwhelm your guests with huge portions. I've eaten my way through twelve-course tasting menus that were so incredibly well thought out, I wasn't left horribly full. I've also experienced the opposite—where I couldn't look at another dish because I was already so full by the tenth course.

- Don't take a big risk and attempt an elaborate new dish for your big dinner party. Cook with confidence. You'll have more fun that way.

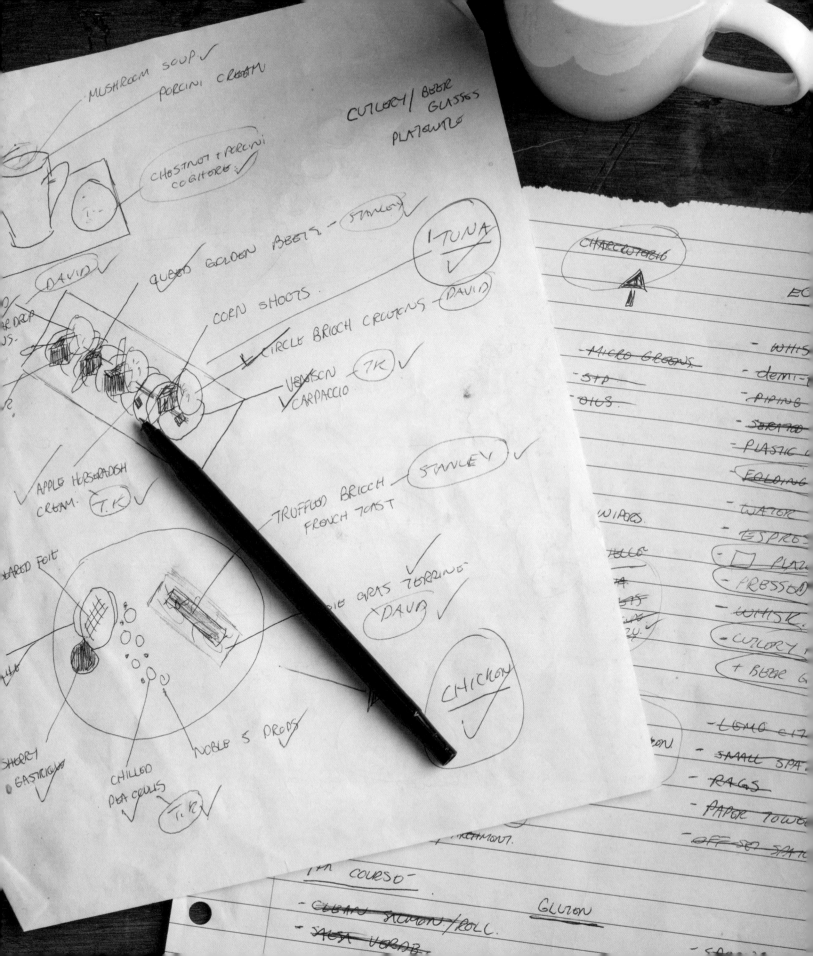

BASICS

Confit Tomatoes

YIELDS 2 PINTS

2 pints (roughly 50) cherry tomatoes
2 sprigs fresh thyme
6 garlic cloves, peeled
4 bay leaves
4 c olive oil

Preheat the oven to 375°F. Place the cherry tomatoes, thyme, garlic and bay leaves into a small ovenproof casserole dish or deep skillet and cover with the olive oil. Bake for 7 to 10 minutes, or until the tomatoes are just beginning to pop. Remove from the oven and set aside.

Dashi Stock

YIELDS 4 CUPS

5-inch square dried kelp (dashi kombu)
5 c cold water
1½ c bonito flakes, loosely packed

Pat kelp dry with paper towels. Fill a medium pot with 4 cups of water, add the kelp and bring to a simmer over medium-high heat. Using a slotted spoon, remove and discard the kelp. Pour in the remaining 1 cup of water to cool off the stock. Add the bonito flakes and bring the mixture back to a simmer. Turn off the heat and allow the dashi to stand for about 5 minutes. Place a piece of cheesecloth over a clean glass jar and strain the dashi through it. Discard the solids. Will keep refrigerated in an airtight container for 2 to 3 days.

Vegetable Stock

YIELDS 6 CUPS

5 large carrots, finely chopped
1 large onion, finely chopped
½ bulb of garlic
2 celery stalks, finely chopped
5 sprigs of thyme
10 sprigs of Italian parsley
10 white peppercorns
1 c white wine
1 c coriander seeds
7½ c water

Place all the ingredients in a large stockpot, bring to a boil over medium heat and cook for 30 minutes. Remove from the heat and allow to cool. Transfer the cooled stock to an airtight container and refrigerate overnight to allow the flavours to develop.

Set a fine chinois over a clean bowl and strain the stock through it. Discard any solids. Once cooled, will keep refrigerated in an air-tight container for up to 5 days or frozen for up to 2 months.

Chicken Stock

YIELDS 8 CUPS

bones from 2 to 3 chickens, chopped

8 c water

1 onion, skin on, roughly chopped

2 celery stalks, roughly chopped

1 large carrot, skin on, roughly chopped

½ bulb of garlic, cut in half

3 sprigs of thyme

8 white peppercorns

2 bay leaves

Wash the chicken bones thoroughly in cold water. Place them and all other ingredients in a large stockpot and bring to a boil over medium heat. Reduce the heat to low and simmer for 2½ hours, using a spoon to skim off any impurities that rise to the surface. Remove from the heat and allow to settle for 30 minutes.

Set a fine chinois over a clean bowl and strain the stock through it. Discard any solids. Once cooled, will keep refrigerated in an airtight container for up to 5 days or frozen in small batches for up to 2 months.

CHEF'S NOTE Gently simmer, never boil stocks, as boiling will make the liquid go cloudy.

Beef Stock

YIELDS 8 CUPS

11 lbs beef bones

3 Tbsp vegetable oil

2 onions, skin on, roughly chopped

3 carrots, skin on, roughly chopped

3 celery stalks, skin on, roughly chopped

1 bulb of garlic, cut in half

6 sprigs of thyme

15 whole black peppercorns

4 Tbsp tomato paste

28 c water

Preheat the oven to 400°F. Place the beef bones in a roasting pan and cook until lightly browned, 1 to 1½ hours. Set aside.

Heat the vegetable oil in a large stockpot over medium-high heat. Add the onions, carrots, celery and garlic and sauté until caramelized, about 15 minutes. Stir in the thyme, peppercorns and tomato paste and cook for another 2 minutes. Add the beef bones and 26 c of water and bring to a simmer.

Place the roasting pan over high heat, add the remaining 2 c of water and, using a wooden spoon, gently release all the caramelized juices and pieces of meat stuck to the bottom of the pan. Pour this liquid into the stockpot and simmer for 5 hours, skimming off any impurities that rise to the surface.

Set a fine chinois over a clean saucepan and strain the stock through it. Discard any solids. Place the stockpot over high heat and cook the stock until reduced to 8 cups. Remove from the heat and allow the stock to cool. Once cooled, will keep refrigerated in an airtight container for up to 5 days or frozen in small batches for up to 2 months.

Classic Brine

YIELDS 4 CUPS

4 c water

2 Tbsp salt

2 garlic cloves, peeled

¼ onion

5 black peppercorns

1 bay leaf

I use this simple brine when I want a moist meat with a neutral flavour. Always make sure to cool the brine before using it, for food safety.

Bring the water to a boil in a large stockpot over high heat. Turn off the heat, add all the remaining ingredients and allow to cool to room temperature. Set a fine-mesh sieve over a clean bowl, then strain the brine. Discard the solids. Will keep refrigerated in an airtight container for up to 10 days.

Spiced Brine

YIELDS 4 CUPS

4 c water

2 Tbsp salt

1 whole star anise

1 garlic clove, crushed

2 strips of lemon zest

5 black peppercorns

1 bay leaf

1 cinnamon stick

1 Tbsp coriander seeds

½ jalapeño pepper, coarsely chopped

This brine is great when you want to kick up the flavour profile of the dish with a little extra zing.

Bring the water to a boil in a large stockpot over high heat. Turn off the heat, add all the remaining ingredients and allow to cool to room temperature. Set a fine-mesh sieve over a clean bowl, then strain the brine. Discard the solids. Will keep refrigerated in an airtight container for up to 10 days.

BASICS

Classic Puff Pastry

YIELDS 1 LB

½ c ice water

1 tsp lemon juice or white vinegar

½ tsp salt

3 Tbsp unsalted butter, melted

1⅓ c + ¼ c all-purpose flour

½ c pastry flour

1 c unsalted butter, room temperature

Use this traditional method when you have more time.

Combine the water, lemon juice or vinegar, and salt in a bowl and mix until the salt is dissolved. Stir in the melted butter.

Place the 1⅓ cups of all-purpose flour and the pastry flour in a bowl and mix well to combine. Pour the flours into a mound on a clean work surface and make a well in the centre. Pour ¾ of the liquid into the centre of the well. Working from the centre outward, use your fingers to draw small amounts of the flour into the liquid. Keep working in the flour in this way until it becomes a paste and then a thick and shaggy dough.

Using a bench scraper or a bowl scraper, cut the dough into smaller pieces, lifting it and folding it as you go. You want to expose as many wet surfaces as possible to evenly incorporate the remaining flour. (Add more liquid, a few drops at a time, only if the dough appears too dry.) The dough should be shaggy, not too sticky, and without any signs of dry flour. Shape the dough into a 5-inch circle, wrap it tightly in plastic wrap and refrigerate for at least 1 hour.

While the dough is resting, place the butter and the ¼ cup of all-purpose flour in a bowl and knead with your hands or a mixer until the flour is evenly distributed throughout the butter. Shape this butter into a 4-inch square, wrap

tightly in parchment paper and refrigerate for at least 30 minutes.

Lightly dust a clean work surface with flour. Remove the dough and the butter from the fridge and make sure they are the same level of firmness. (If the butter is too soft, refrigerate it a bit longer. If it is too firm, leave it on the counter to soften to the same firmness as the dough.) Roll the dough into a 7-inch circle. Place the square of butter in the centre. Using a bench scraper (or a sharp knife), lightly trace the outline of the butter on the dough, then remove the butter and set it aside.

Rolling outward from each side of the outlined square (but not touching it), gently stretch out the dough until you have 4 "flaps," each 3 to 3½ inches long. Unwrap the butter and place it on the dough, then fold each flap over the butter. Do not overlap the flaps of dough; their edges should just meet at a spot in the middle of the butter. Press the edges of the dough together to create a tight seal over the butter. Using a rolling pin and applying even pressure, gently pound the dough at regular intervals until it is 1 inch thick. (Doing this will make the dough malleable and easier to roll. The dough should be cool and flexible, but not soft. If it is too soft, refrigerate it until it is cool. If it is hard, allow it to warm slightly. You want dough that will not crack the butter when it is rolled.)

Lightly dust a clean work surface with flour. Gently roll out the dough to a 5- × 15-inch rectangle, lifting it and adding more flour underneath from time to time to ensure that it does not stick. Brush off all excess flour.

Arrange the rectangle with the short side parallel to the counter. Fold the bottom ⅓ of the dough up and the top ⅓ of the dough down, as if you were folding a letter. Ensure the edges of the dough are lined up neatly and all the corners are square. Turn the dough 90° so the open sides are perpendicular to the counter. This process of rolling, folding and turning is called a single turn. Once you have completed this single turn, dust the pastry block with flour and wrap it in plastic wrap. Refrigerate for a minimum of 30 minutes or up to 24 hours.

Unwrap the pastry, and repeat the folding for five more single turns. Allow to rest refrigerated for a minimum of 1 hour or up to 24 hours. The dough is now ready to use. Or freeze the dough in this state for up to 3 months.

Rough Puff Pastry

YIELDS 1 LB

1 c unsalted butter, frozen, in ½-inch cubes
1½ c all-purpose flour
½ c ice water
1 tsp lemon juice or white vinegar
½ tsp salt

Use this version when you're in a hurry.

In the bowl of a stand mixer fitted with a paddle attachment, combine the butter and flour on low speed until the butter cubes are about ½ their original size.

Combine the ice water, lemon juice or vinegar, and salt in a small bowl and stir until the salt is dissolved. With the motor running, slowly add ¾ of the liquid to the mixer until the dough looks shaggy and barely holds together. Add a few more drops of liquid at a time, if necessary.

Lightly dust a clean work surface with flour. Set the dough on the counter and pat it into a 5-inch square. Roll the dough into a 5- × 15-inch rectangle, lifting the dough and adding more flour underneath, as necessary, to prevent it from sticking. Brush off all excess flour.

Arrange the rectangle with the short side parallel to the counter. Fold the bottom ⅓ of the dough up and the top ⅓ of the dough down, as if you were folding a letter. Ensure the edges of the dough are lined up neatly and all the corners are square. Turn the dough 90° so the open sides are perpendicular to the counter. This process of rolling, folding and turning is called a single turn. Repeat this process for three more single turns. Dust the pastry block with flour and wrap it in plastic wrap. Refrigerate for 1 hour.

Repeat for two more single turns. Allow to rest refrigerated for a minimum of 1 hour or up to 24 hours. The dough is now ready to use. Or freeze the dough in this state for up to 3 months.

 CHEF'S NOTE You can cut the pastry into individual portions before freezing it. Be sure to use a very sharp knife and cut straight down. Don't use any sawing or circular motions, as these will seal and crush the layers you've been working hard to create.

179

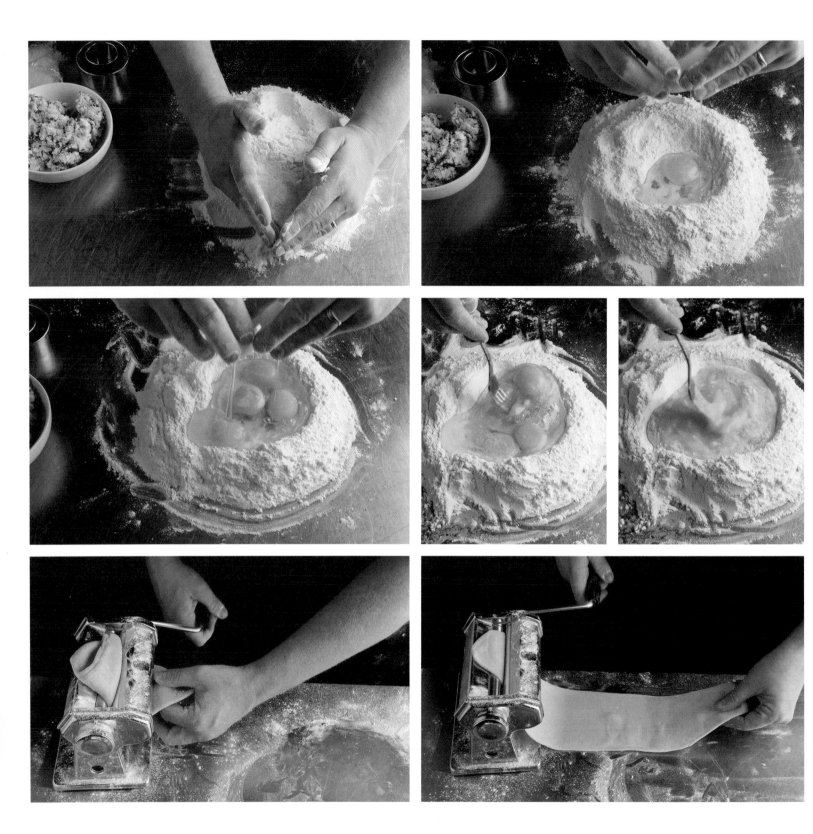

Pasta Dough

SERVES 6 TO 8

1¼ c (180 g or 6.25 oz) tipo "oo" flour
(see Chef's Note)

1¼ c (180 g or 6.25 oz) semola flour
(see Chef's Note)

4 large eggs

1 Tbsp olive oil

Place the "oo" and semola flours into a large bowl, mix well with a fork and make a well in the centre. Crack the eggs into the well and add the olive oil. Using a fork, beat the eggs and oil until smooth.

Working from the centre outward, use the back of the fork to draw small amounts of the flour into the egg mixture. Keep working in the flour in this way until it is completely incorporated.

When you have worked in all the flour—or when you can no longer use the fork to work in the flour—dust both hands with flour. Scoop your dough and any loose flour into a ball. Then using two hands, knead dough for about 5 minutes, or until it becomes smooth, silky and elastic.

To determine whether it is ready for shaping and rolling, use the pinch test. Using your thumb and index finger, pinch through the centre of the dough until your fingertips meet. You know the dough is done when no dough sticks to your fingers when you pull them apart. If dough sticks to your fingers, add a pinch of flour and continue kneading.

Once the dough is ready, cut a large square of plastic wrap. Divide the dough into two parts. Wrap each portion of dough in plastic and set aside while you prepare the pasta machine.

Lightly dust a clean work surface and the pasta machine with flour. Adjust the pasta machine so the rollers are at the widest setting (usually "o"), then unwrap one portion of dough, flatten it slightly and roll it through the pasta machine. Fold the dough over itself and work it through the rollers again. Continue to fold and roll the dough until it feels like suede. Lightly dust the pasta with flour between rollings by setting it on the work surface.

Adjust the pasta machine to the next narrowest setting (usually "1") and pass the dough through the rollers again. Continue to pass the dough through the rollers, adjusting the machine down another setting after each roll. If the dough becomes too long, cut it in half. Keep rolling the pasta until you reach the last or second-to-last setting. Transfer the rolled sheet(s) to a baking sheet and cover each layer with waxed paper. Repeat with the remaining dough.

Once all of the dough has been stacked on the baking sheet, wrap the entire tray tightly with plastic wrap and refrigerate. The rolled dough will keep refrigerated for up to 3 days.

 CHEF'S NOTE Good flour and fresh eggs will make all the difference to the taste and texture of your pasta. Tipo "oo" is a very fine, soft wheat flour traditionally used for making homemade pasta. Semola flour is essentially semolina flour milled extra fine to help add body to your pasta dough. Find them in Italian specialty stores.

METRIC CONVERSION CHART

(ROUNDED OFF TO THE NEAREST WHOLE NUMBER)

Weight

Imperial or U.S.	Metric
1 oz	30 g
2 oz	60 g
3 oz	85 g
4 oz (¼ lb)	115 g
5 oz	140 g
6 oz	170 g
7 oz	200 g
8 oz (½ lb)	225 g
9 oz	255 g
10 oz	285 g
11 oz	310 g
12 oz (¾ lb)	340 g
15 oz	425 g
16 oz (1 lb)	455 g
2 lbs	910 g

Volume

Imperial or U.S.	Metric
⅛ tsp	0.5 mL
¼ tsp	1 mL
½ tsp	2.5 mL
¾ tsp	4 mL
1 tsp	5 mL
½ Tbsp	7.5 mL
1 Tbsp	15 mL
1½ Tbsp	23 mL
⅛ c	30 mL
¼ c	60 mL
⅓ c	80 mL
½ c	120 mL
⅔ c	160 mL
¾ c	180 mL
1 c (½ pint)	240 mL

Linear

Imperial or U.S.	Metric
⅛ inch	3 mm
¼ inch	6 mm
½ inch	12 mm
¾ inch	2 cm
1 inch	2.5 cm
2 inches	5 cm
3 inches	7.5 cm
4 inches	10 cm
5 inches	12.5 cm
6 inches	15 cm
7 inches	18 cm
8 inches	20 cm
9 inches	22.5 cm
12 inches	30 cm
15 inches	37.5 cm
24 inches	60 cm

Oven Temperature

Imperial or U.S.	Metric
39 °F	4 °C
65 °F	18 °C
90 °F	32 °C
95 °F	35 °C
105 °F	41 °C
115 °F	46 °C
125 °F	52 °C
130 °F	54 °C
135 °F	57 °C
140 °F	60 °C
145 °F	63 °C
150 °F	66 °C
155 °F	68 °C
160 °F	71 °C
165 °F	75 °C
170 °F	77 °C
175°F	79°C
180°F	82°C
190°F	88°C
195°F	91°C
220°F	104°C
250°F	120°C
275 °F	135 °C
300 °F	150 °C
325 °F	160 °C
350 °F	180 °C
375 °F	190 °C
400 °F	200 °C
425 °F	220 °C
450 °F	230 °C

Baking utensils

Imperial or U.S.	Metric
9- × 13-inch baking pan	22.5- × 32.5-cm baking pan
12- × 16-inch half sheet pan	30- × 40-cm half sheet pan

The Dirty Apron Cookbook was made possible by the work of a lot of people. First and foremost, I would like to thank the entire team that works so incredibly hard to make the Dirty Apron a place of excellence, culinary excitement and simply a great place to work every day. I feel truly blessed to be surrounded by people as invested, talented and joyful as all of you.

A special thanks to our team of chefs and cooks who have worked tirelessly on this book's recipes, as well as to the front-of-house staff who generously volunteered their time and props for the photography in this book. Takashi Mizukami, Kathrine Tuason, Stanley Yung, Olivia Bailey, Elmark Andres, Joey Armstrong and Ali Ramage: this book wouldn't be the same without your hard work and creative input.

Deepest gratitude also to the people who worked behind the scenes: Lucy Kenward, whose patience and attention to detail have been key to getting all the recipes up to standard; Kerry Gold, whose success in capturing my spoken words and transforming them into the text for this book has far exceeded anything I could have wished for; John Sherlock, whose photographic masterpieces have made these pages truly magical—working with you has been a highlight; Raymond Fryer, whose photo assistance and unparalleled enthusiasm made the photo shoots a joy; and Peter Cocking, whose reputation as the best designer in this country is well deserved—I feel so honoured to have had you dedicate your time to this book.

To the team at Figure 1 Publishing, Chris Labonté, Richard Nadeau and Lara Smith, it's been a pleasure to work with all of you. I am so grateful for the time you took to study and understand the culture that we have worked so hard to build at the Dirty Apron, and for the way in which you have guided everyone involved with this book. Thank you so very much.

My gratitude also to Vikram Vij, for being a supporter of the Dirty Apron since the very beginning and for agreeing to write the foreword to this book. You are one of a kind—and an inspiration to many.

I would also like to thank Kevin Clark for his friendship these past ten years. When we were first starting out in our respective fields, we decided to help each other by working creatively together on food photography: I did the food styling and Kevin took the shots. The front cover image of this book was inspired by a photo shoot that Kevin and I had done many years ago. Thank you, Kevin.

Thank you, John-Carlo Felicella, for seeing and acknowledging my talent and for taking me under your wing, effectively kick-starting my culinary career; to Thomas Henkelmann of the Homestead Inn, for showing me what it truly means to be a chef; and to Nico and Karri Schuermans of Chambar Restaurant, for taking the risk of partnering with me and Sara to start the Dirty Apron. I will always be grateful to you for helping to make my dream of a thriving cooking school come true.

I would like to acknowledge my parents and Sara's who raised us to never give up, to always believe in ourselves and to always give our best. To Vernon and Maureen Robertson: I love you, Mom and Dad, and thank you for always believing in me. To Tom and Monika Reimer, thank you for raising Sara, an incredible woman and business partner, and for allowing me to marry her.

I want to thank John Neate, my business mentor, and my CLC Group, who have been a significant source of support and encouragement to me in the first years of running this business.

I would also like to express my gratitude to my pastors, Dave and Cheryl Koop, whose thoughts and prayers have brought me through the highs and lows of life. And I want to thank God, for his unconditional love, for his guidance and for blessing me far and wide beyond what I deserve. To Him be the glory.

Lastly, I'd like to acknowledge the fact that we are blessed to live in a part of the world that is prosperous and free from oppression. I strongly believe in sharing with people who live in less fortunate conditions. For this reason, the Dirty Apron will donate $1 from the sale of every copy of this book to the Reign Foundation, a charity that helps the people of Cambodia by investing in its future, the children. It currently provides financial support to 151 children, primarily between the ages of six and eight, living in Lvea Em District, Kandal Province, Cambodia. With the help of the foundation, these children have the opportunity to develop the education and life skills they need to create a bright future for themselves, their communities and their country. To learn more about the Reign Foundation and the work it does, visit www.reignfoundation.com.

ADD SOME PROTEIN to your SALAD

INDEX